Introduction

For Teacher:

Table Toppers 1 teaches and reinforces the basic **Addition** and **Su**... while challenging the pupil to remember and apply what has been learned through daily activities and weekly tests.

How to use this book:

- **Learn**   Do one unit each week (**Day 1** on Monday, **Day 2** on Tuesday, **Day 3** on Wednesday and **Day 4** on Thursday).

- **Test**   Friday is Test Day. The last line on **Day 4** of each unit directs the child to the Test page e.g. — '**Do Test 1 on page 62.**' Pupils record their Test Scores on **page 76**.

- **Revision**   These are Revision units in order to revise, consolidate and evaluate progress. Pupils record their Revision Scores on **page 77**.

The Fifty Fivers (at the end of the book) are intended for end-of-year testing.

Tips!

- We strongly recommend reciting the tables at the top of each unit on **Day 1**.

- The secret of teaching tables is to keep it short and sharp, and repeat them every day! Each day's work should take approximately 10 minutes.

- *Table Toppers* is success-based. Less confident children can find all the answers needed at the top of each page in the table box. This allows pupils of every ability to achieve a high level of correct answers. As pupils' proficiency grows, they will no longer need to refer to these answers.

- Where an answer to a sum is provided as an example, it is not to be included in the pupil's score.

- Links to **Tables Games** and IT/IWB activities can be found on **www.cjfallon.ie**.

CJ Fallon

ESTABLISHED 1895

Published by
CJ FALLON
Ground Floor - Block B, Liffey Valley Office Campus, Dublin 22, Ireland

ISBN 978-0-7144-1713-4

©

CJ Fallon

First Edition March 2010
This Reprint May 2022

The paper stock used in this publication comes from managed forests. This means that at least one tree is
planted for every tree felled. The inks used for printing are environmentally friendly and vegetable based.

Printed in Ireland by
Westside Press
Cookstown Industrial Estate
Dublin 24

Contents

Add 1

Day 1 — Say the tables.

		Learn these:
0 + 1 = 1		0 + 1 = 1
1 + 1 = 2		1 + 1 = 2
2 + 1 = 3		2 + 1 = 3
3 + 1 = 4		3 + 1 = 4
4 + 1 = 5		
5 + 1 = 6		
6 + 1 = 7		
7 + 1 = 8		
8 + 1 = 9		
9 + 1 = 10		
10 + 1 = 11		
11 + 1 = 12		
12 + 1 = 13		

1. (a)   1 + 1 = ☐

(b)   3 + ☐ = ☐

(c)   0 + ☐ = ☐

2.
(a)	(b)	(c)	(d)
1	2	0	3
+ 1	+ 1	+ 1	+ 1
☐	☐	☐	☐

3. (a) 2 + 1 = ☐

(b) 3 + 1 = ☐

(c) 0 + 1 = ☐

(d) 1 + 1 = ☐

11

Day 2 — Say the tables.

		Learn these:
0 + 1 = 1		
1 + 1 = 2		
2 + 1 = 3		
3 + 1 = 4		
4 + 1 = 5		4 + 1 = 5
5 + 1 = 6		5 + 1 = 6
6 + 1 = 7		6 + 1 = 7
7 + 1 = 8		
8 + 1 = 9		
9 + 1 = 10		
10 + 1 = 11		
11 + 1 = 12		
12 + 1 = 13		

1. (a)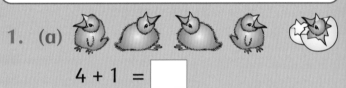

4 + 1 = ☐

(b)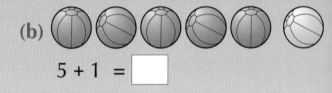

5 + 1 = ☐

(c)   6 + 1 = ☐

2.
(a)	(b)	(c)	(d)
3	5	6	4
+ 1	+ 1	+ 1	+ 1
☐	☐	☐	☐

3. (a) 5 + 1 = ☐

(b) 6 + 1 = ☐

(c) 4 + 1 = ☐

10

Day 3　Say the tables.

Learn these:

$$0 + 1 = 1$$
$$1 + 1 = 2$$
$$2 + 1 = 3$$
$$3 + 1 = 4$$
$$4 + 1 = 5$$
$$5 + 1 = 6$$
$$6 + 1 = 7$$
$$7 + 1 = 8$$
$$8 + 1 = 9$$
$$9 + 1 = 10$$
$$10 + 1 = 11$$
$$11 + 1 = 12$$
$$12 + 1 = 13$$

Learn these:

$$7 + 1 = 8$$
$$8 + 1 = 9$$
$$9 + 1 = 10$$

Day 4　Say the tables.

Learn these:

$$0 + 1 = 1$$
$$1 + 1 = 2$$
$$2 + 1 = 3$$
$$3 + 1 = 4$$
$$4 + 1 = 5$$
$$5 + 1 = 6$$
$$6 + 1 = 7$$
$$7 + 1 = 8$$
$$8 + 1 = 9$$
$$9 + 1 = 10$$
$$10 + 1 = 11$$
$$11 + 1 = 12$$
$$12 + 1 = 13$$

Learn these:

$$10 + 1 = 11$$
$$11 + 1 = 12$$
$$12 + 1 = 13$$

1. (a) $7 + 1 = \boxed{}$

(b) $9 + 1 = \boxed{}$

(c) $8 + 1 = \boxed{}$

2. (a) $\begin{array}{r} 8 \\ + 1 \\ \hline \boxed{} \end{array}$ (b) $\begin{array}{r} 7 \\ + 1 \\ \hline \boxed{} \end{array}$ (c) $\begin{array}{r} 9 \\ + 1 \\ \hline \boxed{} \end{array}$ (d) $\begin{array}{r} 5 \\ + 1 \\ \hline \boxed{} \end{array}$

3. Match.

(a) $7 + 1$ •

(b) $9 + 1$ •

(c) $8 + 1$ •

(d) $6 + 1$ •

7
9
8
10

10

1.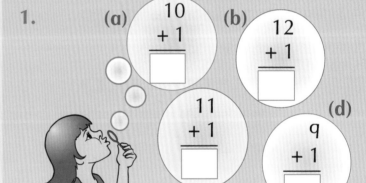

(a) $\begin{array}{r} 10 \\ + 1 \\ \hline \boxed{} \end{array}$ (b) $\begin{array}{r} 12 \\ + 1 \\ \hline \boxed{} \end{array}$

(c) $\begin{array}{r} 11 \\ + 1 \\ \hline \boxed{} \end{array}$ (d) $\begin{array}{r} 9 \\ + 1 \\ \hline \boxed{} \end{array}$

2.

(a) $\begin{array}{r} 10 \\ + 1 \\ \hline \boxed{} \end{array}$ (b) $\begin{array}{r} 12 \\ + 1 \\ \hline \boxed{} \end{array}$ (c) $\begin{array}{r} 7 \\ + 1 \\ \hline \boxed{} \end{array}$ (d) $\begin{array}{r} 11 \\ + 1 \\ \hline \boxed{} \end{array}$

3. (a) $11 + 1 = \boxed{}$

(b) $3 + 1 = \boxed{}$

(c) $12 + 1 = \boxed{}$

(d) $8 + 1 = \boxed{}$

(e) $10 + 1 = \boxed{}$

13

 Do **Test 1** on page **62**.

3

Add 2

Day 1 — Say the tables.

	Learn these:
0 + 2 = 2	0 + 2 = 2
1 + 2 = 3	1 + 2 = 3
2 + 2 = 4	2 + 2 = 4
3 + 2 = 5	3 + 2 = 5
4 + 2 = 6	
5 + 2 = 7	
6 + 2 = 8	
7 + 2 = 9	
8 + 2 = 10	
9 + 2 = 11	
10 + 2 = 12	
11 + 2 = 13	
12 + 2 = 14	

1. (a) 2 + 2 = ☐

(b) 1 + 2 = ☐

(c) 0 + 2 = ☐

(d) 3 + 2 = ☐

2. (a) 3 + 2 = ☐ (b) 1 + 2 = ☐ (c) 0 + 2 = ☐ (d) 2 + 2 = ☐

3. Match.

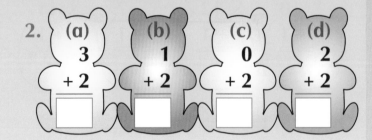

(a) 3 + 2 •   4

(b) 2 + 2 •   2

(c) 0 + 2 •   5   11

Day 2 — Say the tables.

	Learn these:
0 + 2 = 2	
1 + 2 = 3	
2 + 2 = 4	
3 + 2 = 5	
4 + 2 = 6	4 + 2 = 6
5 + 2 = 7	5 + 2 = 7
6 + 2 = 8	6 + 2 = 8
7 + 2 = 9	
8 + 2 = 10	
9 + 2 = 11	
10 + 2 = 12	
11 + 2 = 13	
12 + 2 = 14	

1. (a) 6 + 2 = ☐

(b) 4 + 2 = ☐

(c) 5 + 2 = ☐

2.

(a)	(b)	(c)	(d)
5	6	4	3
+ 2	+ 2	+ 2	+ 2
☐	☐	☐	☐

3. (a) 5 + 2 = ☐

(b) 2 + 3 = ☐

(c) 6 + 2 = ☐

(d) 2 + 2 = ☐

(e) 4 + 2 = ☐

(f) 2 + 1 = ☐   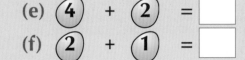 13

Day 3 — Say the tables.

Learn these:

$$0 + 2 = 2$$
$$1 + 2 = 3$$
$$2 + 2 = 4$$
$$3 + 2 = 5$$
$$4 + 2 = 6$$
$$5 + 2 = 7$$
$$6 + 2 = 8$$
$$7 + 2 = 9$$
$$8 + 2 = 10$$
$$9 + 2 = 11$$
$$10 + 2 = 12$$
$$11 + 2 = 13$$
$$12 + 2 = 14$$

Learn these:
$$7 + 2 = 9$$
$$8 + 2 = 10$$
$$9 + 2 = 11$$

1. (a) [image] + [image]

   $8 + 2 = \boxed{}$

   (b) [image] + [image]

   $7 + \boxed{} = \boxed{}$

   (c) [image] + [image]

   $9 + \boxed{} = \boxed{}$

2.
(a)	(b)	(c)	(d)
7	9	8	6
+ 2	+ 2	+ 2	+ 2
$\boxed{}$	$\boxed{}$	$\boxed{}$	$\boxed{}$

3. (a) ⑧ + ② = $\boxed{}$

   (b) ⑦ + ② = $\boxed{}$

   (c) ⑨ + ② = $\boxed{}$

   $\boxed{}$
   `10`

Day 4 — Say the tables.

Learn these:

$$0 + 2 = 2$$
$$1 + 2 = 3$$
$$2 + 2 = 4$$
$$3 + 2 = 5$$
$$4 + 2 = 6$$
$$5 + 2 = 7$$
$$6 + 2 = 8$$
$$7 + 2 = 9$$
$$8 + 2 = 10$$
$$9 + 2 = 11$$
$$10 + 2 = 12$$
$$11 + 2 = 13$$
$$12 + 2 = 14$$

Learn these:
$$10 + 2 = 12$$
$$11 + 2 = 13$$
$$12 + 2 = 14$$

1. (a)  10 + 2 = $\boxed{}$

   (b) 12 + 2 = $\boxed{}$

   (c) 11 + 2 = $\boxed{}$

2. Complete.

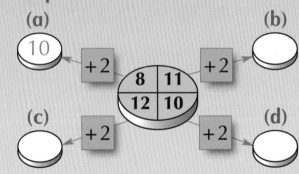

(a) 10 +2
(b) +2
(c) +2
(d) +2

| 8 | 11 |
| 12 | 10 |

3.
(a)	(b)	(c)	(d)
10	9	12	11
+ 2	+ 2	+ 2	+ 2
$\boxed{}$	$\boxed{}$	$\boxed{}$	$\boxed{}$

4. (a) $2 + \boxed{} = 14$

   (b) $2 + \boxed{} = 12$

   $\boxed{}$
   `12`

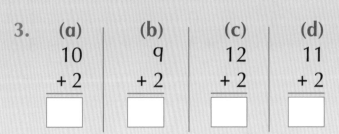

Do Test 2 on page 62.

Add 3

3 4 5 6 7

Day 1 — Say the tables.

					Learn these:				
0	+	3	=	3	0	+	3	=	3
1	+	3	=	4	1	+	3	=	4
2	+	3	=	5	2	+	3	=	5
3	+	3	=	6	3	+	3	=	6
4	+	3	=	7					
5	+	3	=	8					
6	+	3	=	9					
7	+	3	=	10					
8	+	3	=	11					
9	+	3	=	12					
10	+	3	=	13					
11	+	3	=	14					
12	+	3	=	15					

Day 2 — Say the tables.

					Learn these:				
0	+	3	=	3					
1	+	3	=	4					
2	+	3	=	5					
3	+	3	=	6					
4	+	3	=	7	4	+	3	=	7
5	+	3	=	8	5	+	3	=	8
6	+	3	=	9	6	+	3	=	9
7	+	3	=	10					
8	+	3	=	11					
9	+	3	=	12					
10	+	3	=	13					
11	+	3	=	14					
12	+	3	=	15					

Day 1

1.
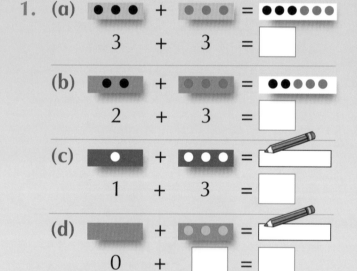

(a) 3 + 3 = ☐

(b) 2 + 3 = ☐

(c) 1 + 3 = ☐

(d) 0 + ☐ = ☐

2.
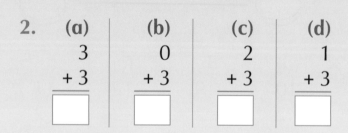

(a) 3
   + 3
   ☐

(b) 0
   + 3
   ☐

(c) 2
   + 3
   ☐

(d) 1
   + 3
   ☐

3.
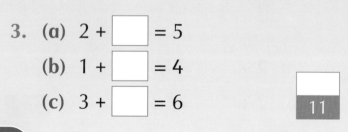

(a) 2 + ☐ = 5

(b) 1 + ☐ = 4

(c) 3 + ☐ = 6

11

Day 2

1.
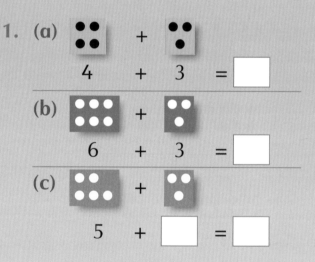

(a) 4 + 3 = ☐

(b) 6 + 3 = ☐

(c) 5 + ☐ = ☐

2.
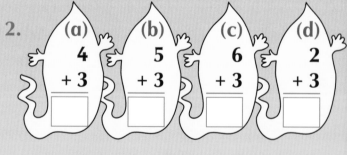

(a) 4
   + 3
   ☐

(b) 5
   + 3
   ☐

(c) 6
   + 3
   ☐

(d) 2
   + 3
   ☐

3. Match.
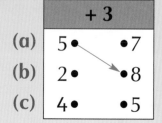

+3	
(a) 5•	•7
(b) 2•	•8
(c) 4•	•5

9

Day 3   Say the tables.

Learn these:

0	+ 3 =	3	
1	+ 3 =	4	
2	+ 3 =	5	
3	+ 3 =	6	
4	+ 3 =	7	
5	+ 3 =	8	
6	+ 3 =	9	
7	+ 3 =	10	7 + 3 = 10
8	+ 3 =	11	8 + 3 = 11
9	+ 3 =	12	9 + 3 = 12
10	+ 3 =	13	
11	+ 3 =	14	
12	+ 3 =	15	

1. (a) 8 + 3 = ☐

(b) 9 + 3 = ☐

(c) 7 + ☐ = ☐

2. (a) 8   (b) 5   (c) 9   (d) 7
    + 3   + 3   + 3   + 3
    ☐   ☐   ☐   ☐

3. (a) 8 + 3 = ☐

(b) 7 + 3 = ☐

(c) 9 + 3 = ☐

Day 4   Say the tables.

Learn these:

0	+ 3 =	3	
1	+ 3 =	4	
2	+ 3 =	5	
3	+ 3 =	6	
4	+ 3 =	7	
5	+ 3 =	8	
6	+ 3 =	9	
7	+ 3 =	10	
8	+ 3 =	11	
9	+ 3 =	12	
10	+ 3 =	13	10 + 3 = 13
11	+ 3 =	14	11 + 3 = 14
12	+ 3 =	15	12 + 3 = 15

1. (a) 10 + 3 = ☐

(b) 12 + 3 = ☐

(c) 11 + 3 = ☐

2. (a) 12   (b) 10   (c) 11   (d) 9
    + 3   + 3   + 3   + 3
    ☐   ☐   ☐   ☐

3. Match.

(a) 8 + 3   8

(b) 7 + 3 •   11

(c) 5 + 3 •   10

10

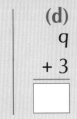

Do Test 3 on page 63.

Add 4

Day 1 — Say the tables.

		Learn these:
0 + 4 = 4		0 + 4 = 4
1 + 4 = 5		1 + 4 = 5
2 + 4 = 6		2 + 4 = 6
3 + 4 = 7		3 + 4 = 7
4 + 4 = 8		
5 + 4 = 9		
6 + 4 = 10		
7 + 4 = 11		
8 + 4 = 12		
9 + 4 = 13		
10 + 4 = 14		
11 + 4 = 15		
12 + 4 = 16		

1. (a)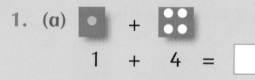

    1 + 4 = ☐

    (b)

    2 + 4 = ☐

    (c)

    3 + ☐ = ☐

2.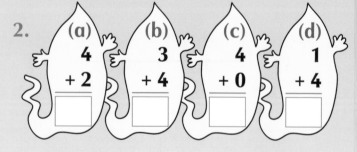

    (a) 4 +2 ☐ (b) 3 +4 ☐ (c) 4 +0 ☐ (d) 1 +4 ☐

3. Match.

    (a) 4 + 2 •   5
    (b) 3 + 4 •   4
    (c) 0 + 4 •   7
    (d) 1 + 4 •   6   11

Day 2 — Say the tables.

		Learn these:
0 + 4 = 4		
1 + 4 = 5		
2 + 4 = 6		
3 + 4 = 7		
4 + 4 = 8		4 + 4 = 8
5 + 4 = 9		5 + 4 = 9
6 + 4 = 10		6 + 4 = 10
7 + 4 = 11		
8 + 4 = 12		
9 + 4 = 13		
10 + 4 = 14		
11 + 4 = 15		
12 + 4 = 16		

1.
(a)	(b)	(c)	(d)
5	6	4	2
+ 4	+ 4	+ 4	+ 4
☐	☐	☐	☐

2.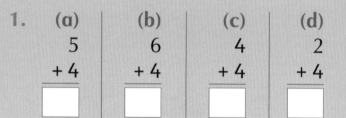

    (a) 4 + 4 = ☐
    (b) 5 + 4 = ☐
    (c) 6 + 4 = ☐
    (d) 3 + 4 = ☐

3. Ring the correct answer.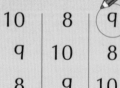

    (a) 4 + 5 =   10   8   ⑨
    (b) 6 + 4 =   9   10   8
    (c) 4 + 4 =   8   9   10
    (d) 4 + 3 =   7   8   9

4. (a) 6 + ☐ = 10

    (b) 4 + ☐ = 8   13

Day 3 Say the tables.

Learn these:

```
0  +  4  =   4
1  +  4  =   5
2  +  4  =   6
3  +  4  =   7
4  +  4  =   8
5  +  4  =   q
6  +  4  =  10
7  +  4  =  11        7  +  4  =  11
8  +  4  =  12        8  +  4  =  12
q  +  4  =  13        q  +  4  =  13
10  +  4  =  14
11  +  4  =  15
12  +  4  =  16
```

Day 4 Say the tables.

Learn these:

```
0  +  4  =   4
1  +  4  =   5
2  +  4  =   6
3  +  4  =   7
4  +  4  =   8
5  +  4  =   q
6  +  4  =  10
7  +  4  =  11
8  +  4  =  12
q  +  4  =  13
10  +  4  =  14       10  +  4  =  14
11  +  4  =  15       11  +  4  =  15
12  +  4  =  16       12  +  4  =  16
```

1. (a) ●●●●●●●● + ●●●●
       8   + 4   = ☐

   (b) ●●●●●●●●● + ●●●●
       q   + 4   = ☐

   (c) ●●●●●●● + ●●●●
       7   + ☐   = ☐

2. Complete.

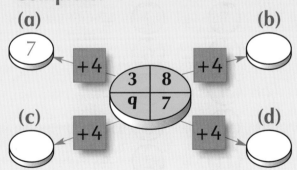

(a) 7 +4
(b) +4
        3 | 8
        q | 7
(c) +4
(d) +4

3. (a) 4 + ☐ = 11

   (b) 8 + ☐ = 12

   (c) 4 + ☐ = 8

   (d) q + ☐ = 13   ☐ / 10

1.

   (a) 12 +4   ☐
   (b) 10 +4   ☐
   (c) q   +4   ☐
   (d) 11 +4   ☐

2. Count on 4.

   (a) 10 | 14   (b) 12 | ☐

   (c) 8 | ☐   (d) 11 | ☐

3. Match.

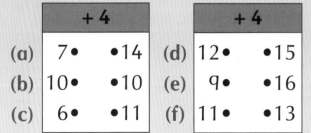

+4			+4	
(a) 7●	●14	(d) 12●	●15
(b) 10●	●10	(e) q●	●16
(c) 6●	●11	(f) 11●	●13

4. (a) 10 + ☐ = 14

   (b) 12 + ☐ = 16   ☐ / 15

Do **Test 4** on page **63**.

Revision A   Addition (+ 1) to (+ 4)

Revision 1

1. (a) ●●●● + ●

   4 + 1 = ☐

   (b) ●●●●●● + ●

   6 + 1 = ☐

   (c) ○○○○○○○ + ○

   7 + 1 = ☐

2.
   (a) 3
   + 1
   ☐

   (b) 5
   + 1
   ☐

   (c) 8
   + 1
   ☐

   (d) 10
   + 1
   ☐

3. Match.

+ 1	
(a) 4●	● 7
(b) 6●	● 5
(c) 9●	●10

+ 1	
(d) 5●	● 3
(e) 10●	● 6
(f) 2●	●11

4. Match.

   (a) 4 + 1 ●   9

   (b) 1 + 8 ●   13

   (c) 9 + 1 ●   5

   (d) 12 + 1 ●   10

5. (a) + = ☐

   (b) + = ☐

   (c) + = ☐

   20

Revision 2

1. (a) ○○○○○ + ●●

   5 + 2 = ☐

   (b) ○○○○○○○○ + ●●

   8 + 2 = ☐

   (c) ○○○○○○ + ●●

   6 + ☐ = ☐

   (d) ●●●●●●●●● + ●●

   ☐ + ☐ = ☐

2. Complete.

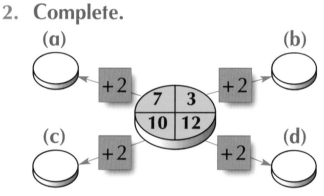

   (a)   (b)

        +2   +2

         7 | 3
        10 | 12

   (c)   (d)

        +2   +2

3.
   (a) 7
   + 2
   ☐

   (b) 9
   + 2
   ☐

   (c) 5
   + 2
   ☐

   (d) 11
   + 2
   ☐

4. (a) ⑤ + ② = ☐

   (b) ② + ⑥ = ☐

   (c) ⑨ + ② = ☐

   (d) ② + ⑧ = ☐

   (e) ⑪ + ② = ☐

5. (a) 6 + ☐ = 8

   (b) 2 + ☐ = 11

   (c) 2 + ☐ = 13

   20

10

Revision 3

1. (a) 6 + 3 = ☐

(b) 8 + 3 = ☐

(c) ☐ + ☐ = ☐

2. (a) 3 (b) 7 (c) 6 (d) 9
   + 3   + 3   + 3   + 3
   ☐   ☐   ☐   ☐

3. Match.

+ 3			+ 3	
(a) 1 •	• 7	(d) 2 •	• 9
(b) 4 •	• 10	(e) 6 •	• 12
(c) 7 •	• 4	(f) 9 •	• 5

4. (a) 6 + ☐ = 9

(b) 3 + ☐ = 5

(c) 3 + ☐ = 12

5. Match.

(a) 5 + 3 •

(b) 8 + 3 •

(c) 10 + 3 •

(d) 0 + 3 •

3
13
8
11

☐
20

Revision 4

1. (a) 5 + 4 = ☐

(b) 8 + ☐ = ☐

(c) 7 + ☐ = ☐

2. (a) 2 (b) 6 (c) 3 (d) 8
   + 4   + 4   + 4   + 4
   ☐   ☐   ☐   ☐

3. Complete.

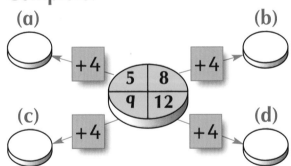

(a) ☐   (b) ☐

+4 5 | 8 +4
    9 | 12

(c) ☐   (d) ☐

+4   +4

4. Match.

+ 4			+ 4	
(a) 2 •	• 8	(d) 6 •	• 13
(b) 4 •	• 6	(e) 10 •	• 10
(c) 8 •	• 12	(f) 9 •	• 14

5. (a) 5 + 4 = ☐

(b) 7 + 4 = ☐

(c) 4 + 11 = ☐

☐
20

Record your **scores** on page **77**. 11

Add 5

5 6 7 8 9

Day 1   Say the tables.

	Learn these:
0 + 5 = 5	0 + 5 = 5
1 + 5 = 6	1 + 5 = 6
2 + 5 = 7	2 + 5 = 7
3 + 5 = 8	3 + 5 = 8
4 + 5 = 9	
5 + 5 = 10	
6 + 5 = 11	
7 + 5 = 12	
8 + 5 = 13	
9 + 5 = 14	
10 + 5 = 15	
11 + 5 = 16	
12 + 5 = 17	

1. (a)

2 + 5 = ☐

(b) 3 + ☐ = ☐

2.

+	(a) 3	(b) 1	(c) 2	(d) 0
5	8			

3.
(a)	(b)	(c)	(d)
5	5	5	5
+ 0	+ 3	+ 2	+ 1
☐	☐	☐	☐

4. (a) ② + ⑤ = ☐

(b) ③ + ⑤ = ☐

(c) ① + ⑤ = ☐

12

Day 2   Say the tables.

	Learn these:
0 + 5 = 5	
1 + 5 = 6	
2 + 5 = 7	
3 + 5 = 8	
4 + 5 = 9	4 + 5 = 9
5 + 5 = 10	5 + 5 = 10
6 + 5 = 11	6 + 5 = 11
7 + 5 = 12	
8 + 5 = 13	
9 + 5 = 14	
10 + 5 = 15	
11 + 5 = 16	
12 + 5 = 17	

1. (a) ▦ + ▦

4 + 5 = ☐

(b) ▦ + ▦

5 + ☐ = ☐

(c) ▦ + ▦

6 + ☐ = ☐

2.
(a)	(b)	(c)	(d)
5	4	3	6
+ 5	+ 5	+ 5	+ 5
☐	☐	☐	☐

3. (a) 4 + 5 = ☐

(b) 5 + 5 = ☐

(c) 6 + 5 = ☐

(d) 5 + ☐ = 9

(e) 5 + ☐ = 11

12

Day 3 Say the tables.

Learn these:

0	+ 5	=	5	
1	+ 5	=	6	
2	+ 5	=	7	
3	+ 5	=	8	
4	+ 5	=	9	
5	+ 5	=	10	
6	+ 5	=	11	
7	+ 5	=	12	7 + 5 = 12
8	+ 5	=	13	8 + 5 = 13
9	+ 5	=	14	9 + 5 = 14
10	+ 5	=	15	
11	+ 5	=	16	
12	+ 5	=	17	

1.
(a) 9 +5 □
(b) 7 +5 □
(c) 8 +5 □
(d) 5 +5 □

2.

	+ 5	
(a)	7	
(b)	6	
(c)	4	

	+ 5	
(d)	8	
(e)	9	
(f)	5	

3. Match.

(a) 9 + 5 •   8
(b) 8 + 5 •   11
(c) 7 + 5 •   14
(d) 5 + 6 •   9
(e) 5 + 3 •   13
(f) 5 + 4 •   12

□   16

Day 4 Say the tables.

Learn these:

0	+ 5	=	5	
1	+ 5	=	6	
2	+ 5	=	7	
3	+ 5	=	8	
4	+ 5	=	9	
5	+ 5	=	10	
6	+ 5	=	11	
7	+ 5	=	12	
8	+ 5	=	13	
9	+ 5	=	14	
10	+ 5	=	15	10 + 5 = 15
11	+ 5	=	16	11 + 5 = 16
12	+ 5	=	17	12 + 5 = 17

1. Complete.

(a)   (b)

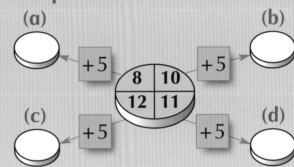

(c)   (d)

2.

(a)	(b)	(c)	(d)
10	9	11	12
+ 5	+ 5	+ 5	+ 5
□	□	□	□

3. Complete. (Add.)

(a) | 3 | + | 5 | = | |
(b) | 11 | + | 5 | = | |
(c) | 9 | | | = | 14 |
(d) | 12 | + | 5 | | |
(e) | 10 | | 5 | | 15 |

□   13

Do **Test 5** on page **64**.

13

Add 6

Day 1 Say the tables.

	Learn these:
0 + 6 = 6	0 + 6 = 6
1 + 6 = 7	1 + 6 = 7
2 + 6 = 8	2 + 6 = 8
3 + 6 = 9	3 + 6 = 9
4 + 6 = 10	
5 + 6 = 11	
6 + 6 = 12	
7 + 6 = 13	
8 + 6 = 14	
9 + 6 = 15	
10 + 6 = 16	
11 + 6 = 17	
12 + 6 = 18	

1. (a) 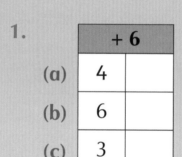 ⚀ + [6 dots]

   1 + 6 = ☐

   (b) [2 dots] + [6 dots]

   2 + ☐ = ☐

   (c) [4 dots] + [6 dots]

   ☐ + ☐ = ☐

2. **Pick the correct answer.**

   8   7   6   9

   (a) 2 + 6 = ☐   (c) 6 + 3 = ☐

   (b) 0 + 6 = ☐   (d) 6 + 1 = ☐

3.

(a)	(b)	(c)	(d)
2	3	1	0
+ 6	+ 6	+ 6	+ 6
☐	☐	☐	☐

11

Day 2 Say the tables.

	Learn these:
0 + 6 = 6	
1 + 6 = 7	
2 + 6 = 8	
3 + 6 = 9	
4 + 6 = 10	4 + 6 = 10
5 + 6 = 11	5 + 6 = 11
6 + 6 = 12	6 + 6 = 12
7 + 6 = 13	
8 + 6 = 14	
9 + 6 = 15	
10 + 6 = 16	
11 + 6 = 17	
12 + 6 = 18	

1.

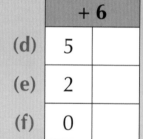

	+ 6			+ 6	
(a)	4		(d)	5	
(b)	6		(e)	2	
(c)	3		(f)	0	

2.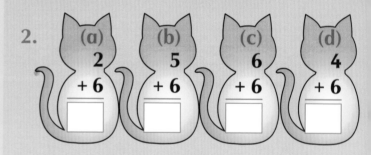

(a)	(b)	(c)	(d)
2	5	6	4
+ 6	+ 6	+ 6	+ 6
☐	☐	☐	☐

3. **Add red balls. Add blue balls.**

5   4   6   6

(a)  ☐ + ☐ = ☐

(b)  ☐ + ☐ = ☐   ☐

12

Day 3 — Say the tables.

Learn these:

```
0  + 6  =  6
1  + 6  =  7
2  + 6  =  8
3  + 6  =  9
4  + 6  =  10
5  + 6  =  11
6  + 6  =  12
7  + 6  =  13          7  + 6  =  13
8  + 6  =  14          8  + 6  =  14
9  + 6  =  15          9  + 6  =  15
10 + 6  =  16
11 + 6  =  17
12 + 6  =  18
```

1. (a)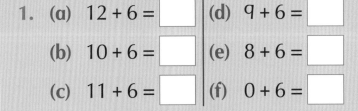

$8 + 6 = \boxed{}$

(b)

$7 + \boxed{} = \boxed{}$

2.
(a)	(b)	(c)	(d)
9	6	7	8
+ 6	+ 6	+ 6	+ 6
□	□	□	□

3. (a) 8 + 6 = □

(b) 9 + 6 = □

(c) 7 + 6 = □

4. ✔ or ✗

(a) 8 + 6 = 12   □

(b) 2 + 6 = 9   □

(c) 9 + 6 = 15   □

`12`

Day 4 — Say the tables.

Learn these:

```
0  + 6  =  6
1  + 6  =  7
2  + 6  =  8
3  + 6  =  9
4  + 6  =  10
5  + 6  =  11
6  + 6  =  12
7  + 6  =  13
8  + 6  =  14
9  + 6  =  15
10 + 6  =  16          10 + 6  =  16
11 + 6  =  17          11 + 6  =  17
12 + 6  =  18          12 + 6  =  18
```

1. (a) $12 + 6 = \boxed{}$ (d) $9 + 6 = \boxed{}$

(b) $10 + 6 = \boxed{}$ (e) $8 + 6 = \boxed{}$

(c) $11 + 6 = \boxed{}$ (f) $0 + 6 = \boxed{}$

2.
(a)	(b)	(c)
□	16	□
11 + 6	10 + □	12 + 6

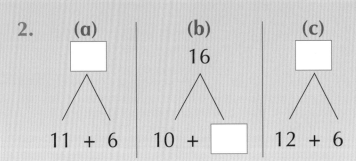

3. Write the correct sums.

| 12 + 6 | 10 + 6 | 11 + 6 |

(a) □ + □ = 17

(b) □ + □ = 16

(c) □ + □ = 18

`12`

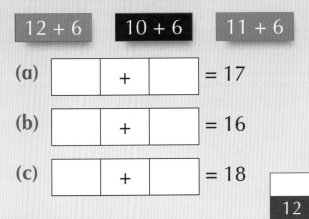

Do **Test 6** on page **64**.

15

Add 7

Day 1 — Say the tables.

	Learn these:
0 + 7 = 7	0 + 7 = 7
1 + 7 = 8	1 + 7 = 8
2 + 7 = q	2 + 7 = q
3 + 7 = 10	3 + 7 = 10
4 + 7 = 11	
5 + 7 = 12	
6 + 7 = 13	
7 + 7 = 14	
8 + 7 = 15	
q + 7 = 16	
10 + 7 = 17	
11 + 7 = 18	
12 + 7 = 19	

1. (a)

    0 + 7 = ☐

(b)

    2 + ☐ = ☐

(c)

    3 + ☐ = ☐

(d)

    ☐ + ☐ = ☐

2.

(a)	(b)	(c)	(d)
1	3	0	2
+ 7	+ 7	+ 7	+ 7
☐	☐	☐	☐

3. (a) 3 + 7 = ☐

   (b) 2 + 7 = ☐

   (c) 0 + 7 = ☐

11

Day 2 — Say the tables.

	Learn these:
0 + 7 = 7	
1 + 7 = 8	
2 + 7 = q	
3 + 7 = 10	
4 + 7 = 11	4 + 7 = 11
5 + 7 = 12	5 + 7 = 12
6 + 7 = 13	6 + 7 = 13
7 + 7 = 14	
8 + 7 = 15	
q + 7 = 16	
10 + 7 = 17	
11 + 7 = 18	
12 + 7 = 19	

1. (a)

    5 + 7 = ☐

(b)

    4 + 7 = ☐

(c)

    6 + 7 = ☐

2.

(a)	(b)	(c)	(d)
4	6	5	3
+ 7	+ 7	+ 7	+ 7
☐	☐	☐	☐

3. Match.

   (a) 6 + 7 •   11
   (b) 4 + 7 •   13
   (c) 5 + 7 •   10
   (d) 3 + 7 •   12   11

Day 3   Say the tables.

Learn these:

0 + 7 = 7		
1 + 7 = 8		
2 + 7 = 9		
3 + 7 = 10		
4 + 7 = 11		
5 + 7 = 12		
6 + 7 = 13		
7 + 7 = 14	7 + 7 = 14	
8 + 7 = 15	8 + 7 = 15	
9 + 7 = 16	9 + 7 = 16	
10 + 7 = 17		
11 + 7 = 18		
12 + 7 = 19		

1. (a)

9 + 7 = ☐

(b)

☐ + ☐ = ☐

2.

(a)	(b)	(c)	(d)
9	7	7	7
+ 7	+ 8	+ 7	+ 6
☐	☐	☐	☐

3. (a) (9) + (7) = ☐

(b) (7) + (7) = ☐

(c) (8) + (7) = ☐

4. **Complete. (Add.)**

(a) | 5 | + | 7 | = | |

(b) | 7 | + | | | 14 |

(c) | 3 | | | = | 10 |

12

Day 4   Say the tables.

Learn these:

0 + 7 = 7		
1 + 7 = 8		
2 + 7 = 9		
3 + 7 = 10		
4 + 7 = 11		
5 + 7 = 12		
6 + 7 = 13		
7 + 7 = 14		
8 + 7 = 15		
9 + 7 = 16		
10 + 7 = 17	10 + 7 = 17	
11 + 7 = 18	11 + 7 = 18	
12 + 7 = 19	12 + 7 = 19	

1.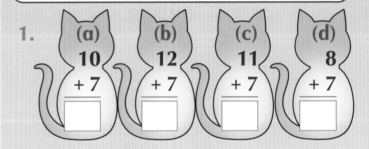

(a) 10 + 7 ☐   (b) 12 + 7 ☐   (c) 11 + 7 ☐   (d) 8 + 7 ☐

2. **Complete.**

(a) ... (b) ...

7	12
11	10

+7   +7   +7   +7

(c) ... (d) ...

3.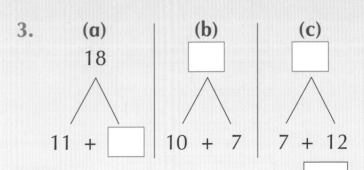

(a) 18 → 11 + ☐

(b) ☐ → 10 + 7

(c) ☐ → 7 + 12

4. 12 + ☐ = 19

12

17

Add 8

Day 1   Say the tables.

					Learn these:				
0	+	8	=	8	0	+	8	=	8
1	+	8	=	q	1	+	8	=	q
2	+	8	=	10	2	+	8	=	10
3	+	8	=	11	3	+	8	=	11
4	+	8	=	12					
5	+	8	=	13					
6	+	8	=	14					
7	+	8	=	15					
8	+	8	=	16					
q	+	8	=	17					
10	+	8	=	18					
11	+	8	=	19					
12	+	8	=	20					

Day 2   Say the tables.

					Learn these:				
0	+	8	=	8					
1	+	8	=	q					
2	+	8	=	10					
3	+	8	=	11					
4	+	8	=	12	4	+	8	=	12
5	+	8	=	13	5	+	8	=	13
6	+	8	=	14	6	+	8	=	14
7	+	8	=	15					
8	+	8	=	16					
q	+	8	=	17					
10	+	8	=	18					
11	+	8	=	19					
12	+	8	=	20					

Day 1

1. (a)

2 + 8 = ☐

(b)

1 + ☐ = ☐

(c)

☐ + ☐ = ☐

2.
(a)	(b)	(c)	(d)
0	1	3	2
+8	+8	+8	+8
☐	☐	☐	☐

3. Complete. (Add.)

(a) | 0 | + | 8 | = | ☐ |

(b) | 3 | + | ☐ | = | 11 |

(c) | 2 | + | ☐ | | 10 |

(d) | 1 | ☐ | ☐ | = | q |

☐ 11

Day 2

1.
(a)	(b)	(c)	(d)
8 +6	4 +8	5 +8	2 +8
☐	☐	☐	☐

2. (a) 14 — 6 + ☐

(b) ☐ — 8 + 4

(c) 13 — 8 + ☐

3. (a) 8 + 6 = ☐

(b) 5 + 8 = ☐

4. Match.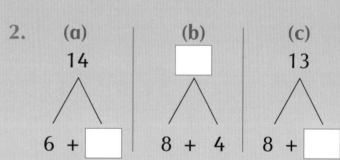

(a) 8 + 6 •   11

(b) 3 + 8 •   13

(c) 4 + 8 •   14

(d) 8 + 5 •   12   ☐ 13

Day 3   Say the tables.

Learn these:

```
 0 + 8 =  8
 1 + 8 =  9
 2 + 8 = 10
 3 + 8 = 11
 4 + 8 = 12
 5 + 8 = 13
 6 + 8 = 14
 7 + 8 = 15          7 + 8 = 15
 8 + 8 = 16          8 + 8 = 16
 9 + 8 = 17          9 + 8 = 17
10 + 8 = 18
11 + 8 = 19
12 + 8 = 20
```

Day 4   Say the tables.

Learn these:

```
 0 + 8 =  8
 1 + 8 =  9
 2 + 8 = 10
 3 + 8 = 11
 4 + 8 = 12
 5 + 8 = 13
 6 + 8 = 14
 7 + 8 = 15
 8 + 8 = 16
 9 + 8 = 17
10 + 8 = 18         10 + 8 = 18
11 + 8 = 19         11 + 8 = 19
12 + 8 = 20         12 + 8 = 20
```

1. (a) 8 + 8 = ☐

(b) 9 + ☐ = ☐

(c) 7 + ☐ = ☐

2. Complete.

(a)   (b)

(c)   (d)

3. (a)   (b)   (c)
   8   7   9
 + 8   + 8   + 8
 ___   ___   ___

10

1. Pick the correct answer.

17   20   16   19   15   18

(a) 8 + 8 = ☐   (d) 8 + 7 = ☐

(b) 12 + 8 = ☐   (e) 9 + 8 = ☐

(c) 8 + 11 = ☐   (f) 8 + 10 = ☐

2. (a)   (b)   (c)   (d)
    10   4   11   12
   + 8   + 8   + 8   + 8
   ___   ___   ___   ___

3. Complete. (Add.)

(a) | 12 | + | 8 | = | |

(b) | 10 | + | | = | 18 |

(c) | 11 | | 8 | = | |

(d) | 9 | | | = | 17 |

(e) | 8 | | 8 | | |

15

Do **Test 8** on page **65**.

19

Revision B — Addition (+ 5) to (+ 8)

Revision 5

1. (a)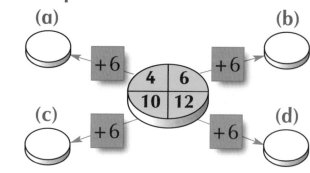

6 + 5 = ☐

(b) 8 + ☐ = ☐

(c) 5 + ☐ = ☐

2.

(a)	(b)	(c)	(d)
4	0	6	q
+ 5	+ 5	+ 5	+ 5
☐	☐	☐	☐

3.

+ 5	
(a) 3	
(b) 5	
(c) 7	

+ 5	
(d) 4	
(e) 8	
(f) 12	

4. (a) 4 + 5 = ☐

(b) 5 + 7 = ☐

(c) 11 + 5 = ☐

5. Match.

(a) 5 + 5

(b) 10 + 5

(c) q + 5

(d) 6 + 5

14
10
11
15

20

Revision 6

1. Complete.

(a)   (b)

4	6
10	12

+6   +6

(c)   (d)

+6   +6

2.

(a)	(b)	(c)	(d)
0	3	7	12
+ 6	+ 6	+ 6	+ 6
☐	☐	☐	☐

3. (a)  3 +  6 = ☐

(b) 6 + 6 = ☐

(c) 6 + 0 = ☐

(d) 6 + q = ☐

4.

(a) q

3 + ☐

(b) ☐

8 + 6

(c) ☐

5 + 6

5. Complete. (Add.)

(a) | 1 | + | 6 | = | |

(b) | 3 | + | 6 | | |

(c) | 6 | + | | = | 11 |

(d) | 8 | | 6 | = | |

(e) | 10 | | | | 16 |

20

20

Revision 7

1. (a)

   3 + 7 = ☐

   (b)

   6 + 7 = ☐

   (c)

   8 + ☐ = ☐

2.
(a)	(b)	(c)	(d)
1	7	6	7
+ 7	+ 3	+ 7	+ 7
☐	☐	☐	☐

3.
	(a)	(b)	(c)	(d)	(e)
+	2	4		9	
7			14		18

4. (a) 3 + 7 = ☐

   (b) 7 + 4 = ☐

   (c) 9 + 7 = ☐

   (d) 10 + 7 = ☐

5. (a) 7 + ☐ = 15

   (b) 10 + ☐ = 17

   (c) 7 + ☐ = 14

   (d) 7 + ☐ = 18

☐ 20

Revision 8

1.
(a)	(b)	(c)	(d)
8	10	12	6
+ 8	+ 8	+ 8	+ 8
☐	☐	☐	☐

2. (a) 3 + 8 = ☐

   (b) 5 + 8 = ☐

   (c) 8 + 7 = ☐

   (d) 9 + 8 = ☐

   (e) 2 + 8 = ☐

3. Complete. (Add.)

   (a)
3	+	8	=	☐

   (b)
5	+	8		☐

   (c)
7			=	15

   (d)
6		8		

   (e)
9				17

4.
(a)	(b)	(c)
10	☐	12
∧	∧	∧
2 + ☐	5 + 8	8 + ☐

5. (a) 8 + ☐ = 15

   (b) 8 + ☐ = 17

   (c) 8 + ☐ = 18

☐ 20

↳ Record your **scores** on page **77**.

21

Add 9

Day 1 Say the tables.

$0 + 9 = 9$
$1 + 9 = 10$
$2 + 9 = 11$
$3 + 9 = 12$
$4 + 9 = 13$
$5 + 9 = 14$
$6 + 9 = 15$
$7 + 9 = 16$
$8 + 9 = 17$
$9 + 9 = 18$
$10 + 9 = 19$
$11 + 9 = 20$
$12 + 9 = 21$

Learn these:

$0 + 9 = 9$
$1 + 9 = 10$
$2 + 9 = 11$
$3 + 9 = 12$

1. (a) $2 + 9 = \boxed{}$

(b) $1 + \boxed{} = \boxed{}$

(c) $\boxed{} + \boxed{} = \boxed{}$

2.
(a) $1 + 9 = \boxed{}$
(b) $2 + 9 = \boxed{}$
(c) $0 + 9 = \boxed{}$
(d) $3 + 9 = \boxed{}$

3. (a) $0 + 9 = \boxed{}$

(b) $2 + 9 = \boxed{}$

(c) $3 + 9 = \boxed{}$

(d) $1 + 9 = \boxed{}$ 11

Day 2 Say the tables.

$0 + 9 = 9$
$1 + 9 = 10$
$2 + 9 = 11$
$3 + 9 = 12$
$4 + 9 = 13$
$5 + 9 = 14$
$6 + 9 = 15$
$7 + 9 = 16$
$8 + 9 = 17$
$9 + 9 = 18$
$10 + 9 = 19$
$11 + 9 = 20$
$12 + 9 = 21$

Learn these:

$4 + 9 = 13$
$5 + 9 = 14$
$6 + 9 = 15$

1. (a) $\boxed{} + \boxed{} = \boxed{}$

(b) $\boxed{} + \boxed{} = \boxed{}$

(c) $\boxed{} + \boxed{} = \boxed{}$

2.
(a) $4 + 9 = \boxed{}$
(b) $3 + 9 = \boxed{}$
(c) $6 + 9 = \boxed{}$
(d) $5 + 9 = \boxed{}$

3. (a) $5 + 9 = \boxed{}$

(b) $6 + 9 = \boxed{}$

(c) $4 + \boxed{} = 13$

(d) $9 + \boxed{} = 14$ 11

Day 3   Say the tables.

Learn these:

0 + 9 = 9
1 + 9 = 10
2 + 9 = 11
3 + 9 = 12
4 + 9 = 13
5 + 9 = 14
6 + 9 = 15
7 + 9 = 16   7 + 9 = 16
8 + 9 = 17   8 + 9 = 17
9 + 9 = 18   9 + 9 = 18
10 + 9 = 19
11 + 9 = 20
12 + 9 = 21

Day 4   Say the tables.

Learn these:

0 + 9 = 9
1 + 9 = 10
2 + 9 = 11
3 + 9 = 12
4 + 9 = 13
5 + 9 = 14
6 + 9 = 15
7 + 9 = 16
8 + 9 = 17
9 + 9 = 18
10 + 9 = 19   10 + 9 = 19
11 + 9 = 20   11 + 9 = 20
12 + 9 = 21   12 + 9 = 21

1. (a)   9 + 9 = ☐

   (b)   7 + ☐ = ☐

   (c)   ☐ + ☐ = ☐

2. (a)   7 + 9 = ☐
   (b)   9 + 9 = ☐
   (c)   8 + 9 = ☐
   (d)   5 + 9 = ☐

3. Match.
   (a) 6 + 9 •   17
   (b) 7 + 9 •   15
   (c) 8 + 9 •   18
   (d) 9 + 9 •   16   11

1.

	+ 9			+ 9
(a)	11		(e)	7
(b)	9		(f)	12
(c)	10		(g)	8
(d)	6		(h)	5

2.

(a)	(b)	(c)	(d)
9	12	10	11
+ 9	+ 9	+ 9	+ 9
☐	☐	☐	☐

3. (a) 10 + 9 = ☐
   (b) 7 + 9 = ☐
   (c) 9 + 9 = ☐
   (d) 12 + 9 = ☐
   (e) 11 + 9 = ☐   17

Do Test 9 on page 66.

23

Add 10

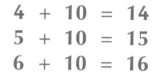

Day 1   Say the tables.

					Learn these:
0	+	10	=	10	0 + 10 = 10
1	+	10	=	11	1 + 10 = 11
2	+	10	=	12	2 + 10 = 12
3	+	10	=	13	3 + 10 = 13
4	+	10	=	14	
5	+	10	=	15	
6	+	10	=	16	
7	+	10	=	17	
8	+	10	=	18	
9	+	10	=	19	
10	+	10	=	20	
11	+	10	=	21	
12	+	10	=	22	

1. (a)   2 + 10 = ☐

   (b)   1 + 10 = ☐

   (c)   3 + 10 = ☐

2.
(a)	(b)	(c)	(d)
2	1	0	3
+ 10	+ 10	+ 10	+ 10
☐	☐	☐	☐

3. Complete. (Add.)

   (a) | 2 | + | 10 | = | ☐ |

   (b) | 0 | + | 10 | | ☐ |

   (c) | 3 | + | ☐ | = | 13 |

   (d) | 1 | | | = | 11 |

   ☐ 11

Day 2   Say the tables.

					Learn these:
0	+	10	=	10	
1	+	10	=	11	
2	+	10	=	12	
3	+	10	=	13	
4	+	10	=	14	4 + 10 = 14
5	+	10	=	15	5 + 10 = 15
6	+	10	=	16	6 + 10 = 16
7	+	10	=	17	
8	+	10	=	18	
9	+	10	=	19	
10	+	10	=	20	
11	+	10	=	21	
12	+	10	=	22	

1.
(a)	(b)	(c)	(d)
4	6	5	2
+10	+10	+10	+10
☐	☐	☐	☐

2. Complete.

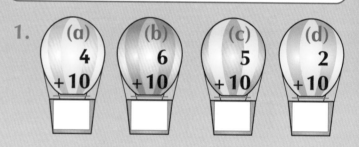

3. Pick the correct answers.

   15   14   16   13

   (a) 10 + 5 = ☐

   (b) 10 + 3 = ☐

   (c) 10 + 6 = ☐

   (d) 10 + 4 = ☐

   ☐ 12

Day 3   Say the tables.

					Learn these:
0	+	10	=	10	
1	+	10	=	11	
2	+	10	=	12	
3	+	10	=	13	
4	+	10	=	14	
5	+	10	=	15	
6	+	10	=	16	
7	+	10	=	17	7 + 10 = 17
8	+	10	=	18	8 + 10 = 18
9	+	10	=	19	9 + 10 = 19
10	+	10	=	20	
11	+	10	=	21	
12	+	10	=	22	

1. (a) 8 + 10 = ☐

(b) 7 + ☐ = ☐

2.

+ 10	
(a) 7	
(b)	19
(c) 6	

+ 10	
(d)	18
(e) 4	
(f) 3	

3. (a) 8 + 10 = ☐

(b) 3 + 10 = ☐

(c) 9 + 10 = ☐

(d) 7 + 10 = ☐   12

Day 4   Say the tables.

					Learn these:
0	+	10	=	10	
1	+	10	=	11	
2	+	10	=	12	
3	+	10	=	13	
4	+	10	=	14	
5	+	10	=	15	
6	+	10	=	16	
7	+	10	=	17	
8	+	10	=	18	
9	+	10	=	19	
10	+	10	=	20	10 + 10 = 20
11	+	10	=	21	11 + 10 = 21
12	+	10	=	22	12 + 10 = 22

1. (a) 10 + 10 = ☐

(b) 12 + 10 = ☐

2. Match. **+ 10**

(a) 7• •21

(b) 11• •20

(c) 10• •17

3.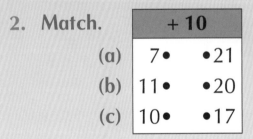

(a) 12 + 10 = ☐ (b) 6 + 10 = ☐ (c) 10 + 10 = ☐ (d) 11 + 10 = ☐

4. ✔ or ✗

(a) 10 + 10 = 21 ☐

(b) 10 + 12 = 22 ☐

(c) 10 + 11 = 12 ☐   12

Do **Test 10** on page **66**.   25

Add 11

Day 1	Say the tables.

	Learn these:
0 + 11 = 11	0 + 11 = 11
1 + 11 = 12	1 + 11 = 12
2 + 11 = 13	2 + 11 = 13
3 + 11 = 14	3 + 11 = 14
4 + 11 = 15	
5 + 11 = 16	
6 + 11 = 17	
7 + 11 = 18	
8 + 11 = 19	
9 + 11 = 20	
10 + 11 = 21	
11 + 11 = 22	
12 + 11 = 23	

1. (a) $1 + 11 = \boxed{}$

(b) $3 + 11 = \boxed{}$

(c) $2 + 11 = \boxed{}$

2.
(a)	(b)	(c)	(d)
1	0	3	2
+ 11	+ 11	+ 11	+ 11
$\boxed{}$	$\boxed{}$	$\boxed{}$	$\boxed{}$

3. (a) $\star 1 \star + \star 11 \star = \boxed{}$

(b) $\star 0 \star + \star 11 \star = \boxed{}$

(c) $\star 3 \star + \star 11 \star = \boxed{}$

(d) $\star 2 \star + \star 11 \star = \boxed{}$

11

Day 2	Say the tables.

	Learn these:
0 + 11 = 11	
1 + 11 = 12	
2 + 11 = 13	
3 + 11 = 14	
4 + 11 = 15	4 + 11 = 15
5 + 11 = 16	5 + 11 = 16
6 + 11 = 17	6 + 11 = 17
7 + 11 = 18	
8 + 11 = 19	
9 + 11 = 20	
10 + 11 = 21	
11 + 11 = 22	
12 + 11 = 23	

1. (a) $6 + 11 = \boxed{}$

(b) $5 + 11 = \boxed{}$

(c) $4 + 11 = \boxed{}$

2. (a) 16
$5 + \boxed{}$

(b) $\boxed{}$
$11 + 6$

(c) 15
$11 + \boxed{}$

3.
(a)	(b)	(c)	(d)
4	3	5	6
+ 11	+ 11	+ 11	+ 11
$\boxed{}$	$\boxed{}$	$\boxed{}$	$\boxed{}$

4. (a) $5 + 11 = \boxed{}$

(b) $4 + \boxed{} = 15$

12

Day 3 Say the tables.

Learn these:

0	+	11	=	11		
1	+	11	=	12		
2	+	11	=	13		
3	+	11	=	14		
4	+	11	=	15		
5	+	11	=	16		
6	+	11	=	17		
7	+	11	=	18	7 + 11 = 18	
8	+	11	=	19	8 + 11 = 19	
9	+	11	=	20	9 + 11 = 20	
10	+	11	=	21		
11	+	11	=	22		
12	+	11	=	23		

1. (a) 4 + 11 ▢ (b) 8 + 11 ▢ (c) 9 + 11 ▢ (d) 7 + 11 ▢

2. Match.

(a) 4 + 11 •   18

(b) 7 + 11 •   15

(c) 9 + 11 •   19

(d) 8 + 11 •   20

3. (a) 9 + 11 = ▢

(b) 7 + 11 = ▢

(c) 8 + 11 = ▢

4. (a) 11 + ▢ = 18

(b) 11 + ▢ = 20

(c) 11 + ▢ = 19   14

Day 4 Say the tables.

Learn these:

0	+	11	=	11		
1	+	11	=	12		
2	+	11	=	13		
3	+	11	=	14		
4	+	11	=	15		
5	+	11	=	16		
6	+	11	=	17		
7	+	11	=	18		
8	+	11	=	19		
9	+	11	=	20		
10	+	11	=	21	10 + 11 = 21	
11	+	11	=	22	11 + 11 = 22	
12	+	11	=	23	12 + 11 = 23	

1. Complete.

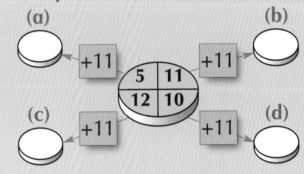

(a)   +11   (b)   +11

| 5 | 11 |
| 12 | 10 |

(c)   +11   (d)   +11

2.
(a)	(b)	(c)	(d)
12	11	9	10
+ 11	+ 11	+ 11	+ 11
▢	▢	▢	▢

3. Complete. (Add.)

(a) | 6 | + | 11 | = | ▢ |

(b) | 10 | + | | = | 21 |

(c) | 12 | | 11 | = | |

(d) | 2 | + | | = | 13 |

(e) | 11 | | | | 22 | ▢

13

Do **Test 11** on page **67**.

Add 12

Day 1 Say the tables.

			Learn these:
0 + 12 = 12			0 + 12 = 12
1 + 12 = 13			1 + 12 = 13
2 + 12 = 14			2 + 12 = 14
3 + 12 = 15			3 + 12 = 15
4 + 12 = 16			
5 + 12 = 17			
6 + 12 = 18			
7 + 12 = 19			
8 + 12 = 20			
9 + 12 = 21			
10 + 12 = 22			
11 + 12 = 23			
12 + 12 = 24			

1. (a) 2 + 12 = ☐

   (b) 3 + 12 = ☐

   (c) 0 + ☐ = ☐

   (d) 1 + ☐ = ☐

2. (a) 12
      + 0
      ☐

   (b) 12
      + 2
      ☐

   (c) 12
      + 3
      ☐

   (d) 12
      + 1
      ☐

3. Complete. (Add.)

   (a) | 0 | + | 12 | = | ☐ |

   (b) | 2 | + | 12 | | ☐ |

   (c) | 3 | + | ☐ | | 15 |

   (d) | 1 | ☐ | ☐ | = | 13 |

   ☐
   12

Day 2 Say the tables.

			Learn these:
0 + 12 = 12			
1 + 12 = 13			
2 + 12 = 14			
3 + 12 = 15			
4 + 12 = 16			4 + 12 = 16
5 + 12 = 17			5 + 12 = 17
6 + 12 = 18			6 + 12 = 18
7 + 12 = 19			
8 + 12 = 20			
9 + 12 = 21			
10 + 12 = 22			
11 + 12 = 23			
12 + 12 = 24			

1. (a) 6 + 12 = ☐

   (b) 4 + ☐ = ☐

2.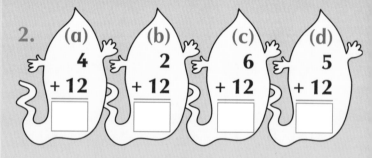

   (a) 4 + 12 ☐

   (b) 2 + 12 ☐

   (c) 6 + 12 ☐

   (d) 5 + 12 ☐

3. ✔ or ✗

   (a) 6 + 12 = 18 ☐

   (b) 4 + 12 = 13 ☐

   (c) 5 + 12 = 15 ☐

4. (a) ⑫ + ⑤ = ☐

   (b) ⑥ + ⑫ = ☐

   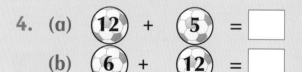

   ☐
   11

Day 3 Say the tables.

Learn these:

```
0  + 12 = 12
1  + 12 = 13
2  + 12 = 14
3  + 12 = 15
4  + 12 = 16
5  + 12 = 17
6  + 12 = 18
7  + 12 = 19      7 + 12 = 19
8  + 12 = 20      8 + 12 = 20
9  + 12 = 21      9 + 12 = 21
10 + 12 = 22
11 + 12 = 23
12 + 12 = 24
```

1. (a) 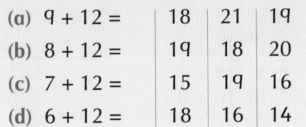 8 + 12 = ☐

(b) 7 + ☐ = ☐

2. Ring the correct answer.

(a) 9 + 12 =   18 | 21 | 19
(b) 8 + 12 =   19 | 18 | 20
(c) 7 + 12 =   15 | 19 | 16
(d) 6 + 12 =   18 | 16 | 14

3. Match.

(a) 7 + 12   18
(b) 6 + 12   21
(c) 9 + 12   19
(d) 8 + 12   16
(e) 4 + 12   20   11

Day 4 Say the tables.

Learn these:

```
0  + 12 = 12
1  + 12 = 13
2  + 12 = 14
3  + 12 = 15
4  + 12 = 16
5  + 12 = 17
6  + 12 = 18
7  + 12 = 19
8  + 12 = 20
9  + 12 = 21
10 + 12 = 22      10 + 12 = 22
11 + 12 = 23      11 + 12 = 23
12 + 12 = 24      12 + 12 = 24
```

1.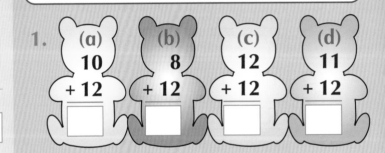
(a) 10 + 12 (b) 8 + 12 (c) 12 + 12 (d) 11 + 12

2. Complete.

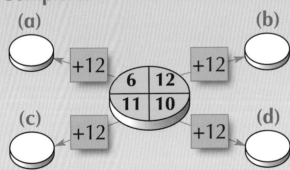

3. (a) 2 + ☐ = 14
(b) 6 + ☐ = 18
(c) 12 + ☐ = 24
(d) 12 + ☐ = 23
(e) 12 + ☐ = 22
(f) 3 + ☐ = 15   14

Do **Test 12** on page **67**.

29

Revision C   Addition (+ 9) to (+ 12)

Revision 9

1.

(a)	(b)	(c)	(d)
8	10	12	4
+ 9	+ 9	+ 9	+ 9
☐	☐	☐	☐

2.

(a) 9 + 9 = ☐

(b) 7 + 9 = ☐

(c) 10 + 9 = ☐

(d) 11 + 9 = ☐

3. Complete. (Add.)

(a) | 1 | + | 9 | = | ☐ |

(b) | 4 | + | 9 | | ☐ |

(c) | 6 | | 9 | = | ☐ |

(d) | 9 | + | ☐ | | 18 |

(e) | 12 | | 9 | = | ☐ |

4.

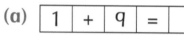

(a)	(b)	(c)
☐	11	14
0 + 9	9 + ☐	5 + ☐

5. Match.

+ 9	
(a) 4 •	• 15
(b) 8 •	• 11
(c) 6 •	• 13
(d) 2 •	• 17

☐

20

Revision 10

1.

	+ 10	
(a)	7	
(b)		20
(c)		18
(d)	12	

2.

(a)	(b)	(c)	(d)
8	10	12	7
+ 10	+ 10	+ 10	+ 10
☐	☐	☐	☐

3.

(a) 5 + 10 = ☐

(b) 4 + 10 = ☐

(c) 8 + 10 = ☐

(d) 10 + 10 = ☐

4. Match.

(a) 10 + 1 •   19

(b) 10 + 8 •   18

(c) 10 + 6 •   11

(d) 10 + 9 •   16

5. (a) 10 + ☐ = 13

(b) 7 + ☐ = 17

(c) 10 + ☐ = 20

(d) 10 + ☐ = 15

☐

20

Revision 11

1. Complete.

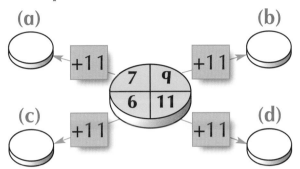

   (a)   (b)   (c)   (d)

   +11   +11   +11   +11

   7 9
   6 11

2. Ring the correct answer.

   (a) 11 + 2 = | 12 | 13 | 14
   (b) 11 + 10 = | 21 | 22 | 23
   (c) 7 + 11 = | 18 | 20 | 21
   (d) 11 + 9 = | 17 | 19 | 20

3.
   (a)   (b)   (c)   (d)
   3   11   8   11
   + 11   + 7   + 11   + 0
   ☐   ☐   ☐   ☐

4.
   (a)   (b)   (c)
   ☐   16   ☐
   /\   /\   /\
   11 + 3   11 + ☐   7 + 11

5. (a) 11 + 5 = ☐
   (b) 2 + 11 = ☐
   (c) 11 + 6 = ☐
   (d) 9 + 11 = ☐
   (e) 11 + 10 = ☐ ☐

20

Revision 12

1. (a) ●●●● + ●●●●●●●●●●●●
      4 + 12 = ☐

   (b) ●●●●●● + ●●●●●●●●●●●●
      6 + ☐ = ☐

   (c) ●●●●●●●● + ●●●●●●●●●●●●
      ☐ + ☐ = ☐

2.
   (a)   (b)   (c)   (d)
   12   5   12   12
   + 3   + 12   + 7   + 11
   ☐   ☐   ☐   ☐

3.
	(a)	(b)	(c)	(d)	(e)
+	3	5		11	9
12			16		

4. Complete. (Add.)

   (a) | 2 | + | 12 | = | ☐ |
   (b) | 5 | + | ☐ | = | 17 |
   (c) | 8 | | 12 | | ☐ |
   (d) | 9 | | ☐ | = | 21 |
   (e) | 12 | | 12 | = | ☐ |

5. (a) 4 + ☐ = 16
   (b) 12 + ☐ = 24
   (c) 12 + ☐ = 14

20

Subtract 1

Day 1　Say the tables.

				Learn these:
1	–	1	=	0
2	–	1	=	1
3	–	1	=	2
4	–	1	=	3
5	–	1	=	4
6	–	1	=	5
7	–	1	=	6
8	–	1	=	7
9	–	1	=	8
10	–	1	=	9
11	–	1	=	10
12	–	1	=	11
13	–	1	=	12

Learn these:
1 – 1 = 0
2 – 1 = 1
3 – 1 = 2
4 – 1 = 3

Day 2　Say the tables.

				Learn these:
1	–	1	=	0
2	–	1	=	1
3	–	1	=	2
4	–	1	=	3
5	–	1	=	4
6	–	1	=	5
7	–	1	=	6
8	–	1	=	7
9	–	1	=	8
10	–	1	=	9
11	–	1	=	10
12	–	1	=	11
13	–	1	=	12

Learn these:
5 – 1 = 4
6 – 1 = 5
7 – 1 = 6

---

1. (a)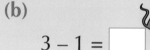

   $4 - 1 = \boxed{}$

   (b)

   $3 - 1 = \boxed{}$

   (c)

   $2 - 1 = \boxed{}$

   (d)

   $1 - 1 = \boxed{}$　

2. (a) $0 + \boxed{} = 1$, so $1 - 1 = \boxed{}$

   (b) $1 + \boxed{} = 2$, so $2 - 1 = \boxed{}$

   (c) $2 + \boxed{} = 3$, so $3 - 1 = \boxed{}$

   (d) $3 + \boxed{} = 4$, so $4 - 1 = \boxed{}$

3.

(a)	(b)	(c)
3	4	2
– 1	– 1	– 1
$\boxed{}$	$\boxed{}$	$\boxed{}$

11

---

1. (a)

   $5 - 1 = \boxed{}$

   (b)

   $6 - 1 = \boxed{}$

   (c)

   $7 - 1 = \boxed{}$

2.

(a)	(b)	(c)	(d)
5	6	4	7
– 1	– 1	– 1	– 1
$\boxed{}$	$\boxed{}$	$\boxed{}$	$\boxed{}$

3. (a) 6 – 1 = $\boxed{}$

   (b) 7 – 1 = $\boxed{}$

   (c)  5 – 1 = $\boxed{}$

   10

Day 3 — Say the tables.

Learn these:

1	– 1	=	0	
2	– 1	=	1	
3	– 1	=	2	
4	– 1	=	3	
5	– 1	=	4	
6	– 1	=	5	
7	– 1	=	6	
8	– 1	=	7	8 – 1 = 7
9	– 1	=	8	9 – 1 = 8
10	– 1	=	9	10 – 1 = 9
11	– 1	=	10	
12	– 1	=	11	
13	– 1	=	12	

1. (a)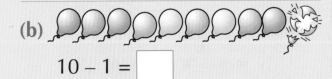

  9 – 1 = ☐

  (b)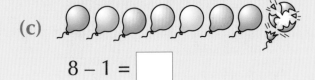

  10 – 1 = ☐

  (c)

  8 – 1 = ☐

2. (a) 8 + ☐ = 9, so 9 – 1 = ☐

  (b) 7 + ☐ = 8, so 8 – 1 = ☐

  (c) 9 + ☐ = 10, so 10 – 1 = ☐

  (d) 6 + ☐ = 7, so 7 – 1 = ☐

3.

  (a) 9 – 1   (b) 10 – 1   (c) 8 – 1

  ☐ 10

Day 4 — Say the tables.

Learn these:

1	– 1	=	0	
2	– 1	=	1	
3	– 1	=	2	
4	– 1	=	3	
5	– 1	=	4	
6	– 1	=	5	
7	– 1	=	6	
8	– 1	=	7	
9	– 1	=	8	
10	– 1	=	9	
11	– 1	=	10	11 – 1 = 10
12	– 1	=	11	12 – 1 = 11
13	– 1	=	12	13 – 1 = 12

1. (a) 12 + ☐ = 13, so 13 – 1 = ☐

  (b) 10 + ☐ = 11, so 11 – 1 = ☐

  (c) 11 + ☐ = 12, so 12 – 1 = ☐

2.

	– 1				– 1	
(a)	8	7		(e)	5	
(b)	10			(f)	11	
(c)	7			(g)	9	
(d)	12			(h)	13	

3. Count back 1.

  (a)  10 11

  (b)  ☐ 13

  (c) ☐ 10

  (d)  ☐ 12

4. 12 – ☐ = 11

  ☐ 14

Do Test 13 on page 68.

Subtract 2

Day 1 Say the tables.

	Learn these:
2 – 2 = 0	2 – 2 = 0
3 – 2 = 1	3 – 2 = 1
4 – 2 = 2	4 – 2 = 2
5 – 2 = 3	5 – 2 = 3
6 – 2 = 4	
7 – 2 = 5	
8 – 2 = 6	
9 – 2 = 7	
10 – 2 = 8	
11 – 2 = 9	
12 – 2 = 10	
13 – 2 = 11	
14 – 2 = 12	

1. (a) 4 – 2 = ☐

(b) 3 – 2 = ☐

(c) 5 – ☐ = ☐

(d) 2 – 2 = ☐

2.
(a)	(b)	(c)	(d)
5	4	2	3
– 2	– 2	– 2	– 2
☐	☐	☐	☐

3. Count back 2.

(a) ☐ 5

(b) ☐ 2

(c) ☐ 4

(d) ☐ 3

4. (a) 4 – 2 = ☐

(b) 3 – 2 = ☐   ☐

14

Day 2 Say the tables.

	Learn these:
2 – 2 = 0	
3 – 2 = 1	
4 – 2 = 2	
5 – 2 = 3	
6 – 2 = 4	6 – 2 = 4
7 – 2 = 5	7 – 2 = 5
8 – 2 = 6	8 – 2 = 6
9 – 2 = 7	
10 – 2 = 8	
11 – 2 = 9	
12 – 2 = 10	
13 – 2 = 11	
14 – 2 = 12	

1. (a) 6 – 2 = ☐

(b) 5 – 2 = ☐

(c) 7 – 2 = ☐

(d) 8 – 2 = ☐

2.
– 2	
(a) 8	
(b) 6	
(c) 4	

– 2	
(d) 7	
(e) 3	
(f) 2	

3. (a) 6 + 2 = ☐, so 8 – 2 = ☐

(b) 4 + 2 = ☐, so 6 – 2 = ☐

4. (a) 8 – 2 = ☐

(b) 7 – 2 = ☐   ☐

(c) 6 – 2 = ☐   15

Day 3 Say the tables.

Learn these:

2 – 2 = 0	
3 – 2 = 1	
4 – 2 = 2	
5 – 2 = 3	
6 – 2 = 4	
7 – 2 = 5	
8 – 2 = 6	
9 – 2 = 7	9 – 2 = 7
10 – 2 = 8	10 – 2 = 8
11 – 2 = 9	11 – 2 = 9
12 – 2 = 10	
13 – 2 = 11	
14 – 2 = 12	

1. (a)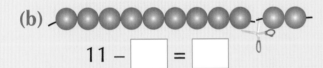

9 – 2 = ☐

(b)

11 – ☐ = ☐

2. Match.

(a) 7 – 2

(b) 9 – 2

(c) 11 – 2

(d) 10 – 2

| 7 |
| 8 |
| 5 |
| 9 |

3.
(a)	(b)	(c)	(d)
11	9	7	10
– 2	– 2	– 2	– 2
☐	☐	☐	☐

4. (a) 9 – ☐ = 7   ☐

   (b) 10 – ☐ = 8   12

Day 4 Say the tables.

Learn these:

2 – 2 = 0	
3 – 2 = 1	
4 – 2 = 2	
5 – 2 = 3	
6 – 2 = 4	
7 – 2 = 5	
8 – 2 = 6	
9 – 2 = 7	
10 – 2 = 8	
11 – 2 = 9	
12 – 2 = 10	12 – 2 = 10
13 – 2 = 11	13 – 2 = 11
14 – 2 = 12	14 – 2 = 12

1.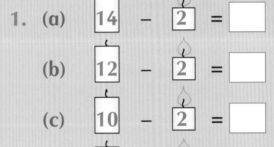

(a) 14 – 2 = ☐

(b) 12 – 2 = ☐

(c) 10 – 2 = ☐

(d) 13 – 2 = ☐

2.
(a)	(b)	(c)	(d)
7	12	14	13
– 2	– 2	– 2	– 2
☐	☐	☐	☐

3.
	– 2
(a) 13	
(b) 10	
(c) 14	
(d) 12	

☐
12

Do **Test 14** on page **68**.

Subtract 3

3 | 4 | 5 | 6 | 7

Day 1 — Say the tables.

	Learn these:
3 – 3 = 0	3 – 3 = 0
4 – 3 = 1	4 – 3 = 1
5 – 3 = 2	5 – 3 = 2
6 – 3 = 3	6 – 3 = 3
7 – 3 = 4	
8 – 3 = 5	
9 – 3 = 6	
10 – 3 = 7	
11 – 3 = 8	
12 – 3 = 9	
13 – 3 = 10	
14 – 3 = 11	
15 – 3 = 12	

1. (a) 6 – 3 = ☐

(b) 4 – 3 = ☐

(c) 3 – 3 = ☐

(d) 5 – 3 = ☐

2.

(a)	(b)	(c)	(d)
3	6	5	4
– 3	– 3	– 3	– 3
☐	☐	☐	☐

3. (a) 6 – 3 = ☐

(b) 5 – 3 = ☐

(c) 4 – 3 = ☐

(d) 3 – 3 = ☐

12

Day 2 — Say the tables.

	Learn these:
3 – 3 = 0	
4 – 3 = 1	
5 – 3 = 2	
6 – 3 = 3	
7 – 3 = 4	7 – 3 = 4
8 – 3 = 5	8 – 3 = 5
9 – 3 = 6	9 – 3 = 6
10 – 3 = 7	
11 – 3 = 8	
12 – 3 = 9	
13 – 3 = 10	
14 – 3 = 11	
15 – 3 = 12	

1. (a) 9 – 3 = ☐

(b) 8 – 3 = ☐

(c) 7 – 3 = ☐

2. (a) 3 + ☐ = 7, so 7 – 3 = ☐

(b) 3 + ☐ = 9, so 9 – 3 = ☐

(c) 3 + ☐ = 8, so 8 – 3 = ☐

(d) 3 + ☐ = 5, so 5 – 3 = ☐

3.

(a)	(b)	(c)	(d)
9	5	7	8
– 3	– 3	– 3	– 3
☐	☐	☐	☐

4. Complete. (Subtract.)

(a) | 9 | – | 3 | = | ☐ |

(b) | 8 | ☐ | ☐ | = | 5 |

(c) | 7 | – | ☐ | | 4 |

14

Day 3　Say the tables.

Learn these:

3 − 3 = 0
4 − 3 = 1
5 − 3 = 2
6 − 3 = 3
7 − 3 = 4
8 − 3 = 5
q − 3 = 6
10 − 3 = 7 　　　10 − 3 = 7
11 − 3 = 8 　　　11 − 3 = 8
12 − 3 = q 　　　12 − 3 = q
13 − 3 = 10
14 − 3 = 11
15 − 3 = 12

1. (a)  12 − 3 = ☐

(b) 10 − ☐ = 7

(c) 11 − ☐ = ☐

2. Complete.

(a) ④ —−3→ 　　　　　　(b) —−3→ ◯

7 | 10
11 | 12

(c) ◯ ←−3— 　　　　　　(d) —−3→ ◯

3. Fill in the gaps.

(a) 10 −3→ 7 −3→ ☐

(b) 12 −3→ ☐ −3→ ☐

(c) 11 −3→ ☐ −3→ ☐　　☐
　　　　　　　　　　　　　q

Day 4　Say the tables.

Learn these:

3 − 3 = 0
4 − 3 = 1
5 − 3 = 2
6 − 3 = 3
7 − 3 = 4
8 − 3 = 5
q − 3 = 6
10 − 3 = 7
11 − 3 = 8
12 − 3 = q
13 − 3 = 10 　　　13 − 3 = 10
14 − 3 = 11 　　　14 − 3 = 11
15 − 3 = 12 　　　15 − 3 = 12

1. (a)  13 − 3 = ☐

(b) 15 − 3 = ☐

(c) 14 − ☐ = 11

2. (a)  14 − 3 = ☐

(b) 13 − 3 = ☐

(c) 15 − 3 = ☐

3. Complete. (Subtract.)

(a) | 13 | − | 3 | = | ☐ |

(b) | q | | 3 | = | ☐ |

(c) | 14 | | 3 | | 11 |

(d) | 15 | − | ☐ | | 12 |

4. (a) 13 − ☐ = 10

(b) 15 − ☐ = 12
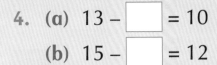
　　　　　　　　　　　　☐
　　　　　　　　　　　　12

Do Test 15 on page 69.

Subtract 4

Day 1   Say the tables.

		Learn these:
4 – 4 = 0	4 – 4 = 0
5 – 4 = 1	5 – 4 = 1
6 – 4 = 2	6 – 4 = 2
7 – 4 = 3	7 – 4 = 3
8 – 4 = 4	
9 – 4 = 5	
10 – 4 = 6	
11 – 4 = 7	
12 – 4 = 8	
13 – 4 = 9	
14 – 4 = 10	
15 – 4 = 11	
16 – 4 = 12	

1. (a) 6 – 4 = ☐

(b) 5 – 4 = ☐

(c) 4 – 4 = ☐

(d) 7 – ☐ = ☐

2.
(a)	(b)	(c)	(d)
5	7	4	6
– 4	– 4	– 4	– 4
☐	☐	☐	☐

3. (a) 7 – 4 = ☐

(b) 4 – 4 = ☐

(c) 6 – 4 = ☐

(d) 5 – 4 = ☐   12

Day 2   Say the tables.

		Learn these:
4 – 4 = 0	
5 – 4 = 1	
6 – 4 = 2	
7 – 4 = 3	
8 – 4 = 4	8 – 4 = 4
9 – 4 = 5	9 – 4 = 5
10 – 4 = 6	10 – 4 = 6
11 – 4 = 7	
12 – 4 = 8	
13 – 4 = 9	
14 – 4 = 10	
15 – 4 = 11	
16 – 4 = 12	

1. (a) 5 – ☐ = ☐

(b) 8 – ☐ = ☐

(c) 9 – ☐ = ☐

(d) 10 – ☐ = ☐

2.
(a)	(b)	(c)	(d)
9	7	10	8
– 4	– 4	– 4	– 4
☐	☐	☐	☐

3. (a) 9 – 4 = ☐

(b) 8 – 4 = ☐

(c) 10 – 4 = ☐

(d) 6 – 4 = ☐   12

Day 3 Say the tables.

Learn these:

$$4 - 4 = 0$$
$$5 - 4 = 1$$
$$6 - 4 = 2$$
$$7 - 4 = 3$$
$$8 - 4 = 4$$
$$q - 4 = 5$$
$$10 - 4 = 6$$
$$11 - 4 = 7 \qquad 11 - 4 = 7$$
$$12 - 4 = 8 \qquad 12 - 4 = 8$$
$$13 - 4 = q \qquad 13 - 4 = q$$
$$14 - 4 = 10$$
$$15 - 4 = 11$$
$$16 - 4 = 12$$

Day 4 Say the tables.

Learn these:

$$4 - 4 = 0$$
$$5 - 4 = 1$$
$$6 - 4 = 2$$
$$7 - 4 = 3$$
$$8 - 4 = 4$$
$$q - 4 = 5$$
$$10 - 4 = 6$$
$$11 - 4 = 7$$
$$12 - 4 = 8$$
$$13 - 4 = q$$
$$14 - 4 = 10 \qquad 14 - 4 = 10$$
$$15 - 4 = 11 \qquad 15 - 4 = 11$$
$$16 - 4 = 12 \qquad 16 - 4 = 12$$

1. (a) $11 - 4 = \boxed{}$

(b) $13 - \boxed{} = \boxed{}$

(c) $12 - \boxed{} = \boxed{}$

2. Match.

(a) $13 - 4$ •

(b) $11 - 4$ •

(c) $q - 4$ •

(d) $12 - 4$ •

| 5 |
| 7 |
| 8 |
| q |

3. ✔ **or** ✗

(a) $11 - 4 = 8$ $\boxed{}$

(b) $12 - 4 = 8$ $\boxed{}$

(c) $13 - 4 = 7$ $\boxed{}$

(d) $q - 4 = 5$ $\boxed{}$

| 11 |

1. (a) $16 - 4 = \boxed{}$

(b) $14 - \boxed{} = \boxed{}$

(c) $15 - \boxed{} = \boxed{}$

2. Complete.

(a)  (b)

(c) (d)

-4 -4
| 8 | 16 |
| 15 | 14 |
-4 -4

3. (a) $14 - \boxed{} = 10$

(b) $16 - \boxed{} = 12$

| q |

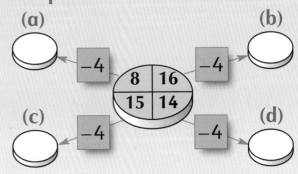

Do **Test 16** on page **69**.

Revision 13

1. (a)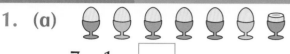

   7 − 1 = ☐

   (b)

   8 − ☐ = ☐

   (c)

   ☐ − ☐ = ☐

   (d)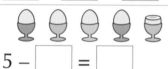

   5 − ☐ = ☐

2.

− 1	
(a) 4	
(b) 7	
(c) 6	

− 1	
(d) 8	
(e) 11	
(f) 9	

3. (a) 6 + 1 = ☐ , so 7 − 1 = ☐

   (b) 9 + 1 = ☐ , so 10 − 1 = ☐

   (c) 12 + 1 = ☐ , so 13 − 1 = ☐

   (d) 10 + 1 = ☐ , so 11 − 1 = ☐

   (e) 7 + 1 = ☐ , so 8 − 1 = ☐

4. Count back 1.

   (a) | 5

   (b) | 13

5.

	(a)	(b)	(c)
	5	10	12
	− 1	− 1	− 1
	☐	☐	☐

20

Revision 14

1. (a)

   7 − 2 = ☐

   (b)

   9 − ☐ = ☐

   (c)

   5 − ☐ = ☐

   (d)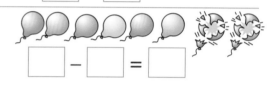

   ☐ − ☐ = ☐

2.

(a)	(b)	(c)	(d)
4	5	11	9
− 2	− 2	− 2	− 2
☐	☐	☐	☐

3. (a) 3 − 2 = ☐

   (b) 12 − 2 = ☐

   (c) 8 − 2 = ☐

4. Count back 2.

   (a) | 4   (b) ☐ | 7

   (c) ☐ | 6   (d) ☐ | 12

5. Match.

   (a) 10 − 2 •   10

   (b)   8 − 2 •   7

   (c) 12 − 2 •   8

   (d)   6 − 2 •   6

   (e)   9 − 2 •   4

20

1. (a) 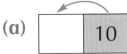 7 − 3 = ☐

(b) 9 − 3 = ☐

2.
(a) 6 − 3 ☐
(b) 9 − 3 ☐
(c) 8 − 3 ☐
(d) 11 − 3 ☐

3. Count back 3.

(a) ☐ 10   (b) ☐ 14

4. Match.

(a) 7 − 3 •   2
(b) 4 − 3 •   9
(c) 10 − 3 •   7
(d) 5 − 3 •   4
(e) 12 − 3 •   1

5. (a) 11 − 3 = ☐
(b) 13 − 3 = ☐
(c) 12 − 3 = ☐
(d) 8 − 3 = ☐

6. Complete. (Subtract.)

(a) 8 − 3 = ☐
(b) 4 − 3 = ☐
(c) 9 ☐ = 6

20

1. (a) 8 − 4 = ☐

(b) 7 − ☐ = ☐

(c) ☐ − ☐ = ☐

2. Complete.

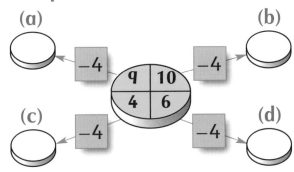

(a)   (b)

−4   9 | 10   −4
       4 | 6

(c) −4   −4 (d)

3.
(a) 5 − 4 ☐
(b) 8 − 4 ☐
(c) 7 − 4 ☐
(d) 12 − 4 ☐

4. (a) 8 + ☐ = 12, so 12 − ☐ = 8
(b) 6 + ☐ = 10, so 10 − ☐ = 6
(c) 5 + ☐ = 9, so 9 − ☐ = 5
(d) 3 + ☐ = 7, so 7 − ☐ = 3
(e) 7 + ☐ = 11, so 11 − ☐ = 7

5. (a) 4 − 4 = ☐
(b) 9 − 4 = ☐
(c) 11 − 4 = ☐
(d) 8 − 4 = ☐

20

Subtract 5

Day 1 Say the tables.

Learn these:

5 – 5 = 0	5 – 5 = 0
6 – 5 = 1	6 – 5 = 1
7 – 5 = 2	7 – 5 = 2
8 – 5 = 3	8 – 5 = 3
9 – 5 = 4	
10 – 5 = 5	
11 – 5 = 6	
12 – 5 = 7	
13 – 5 = 8	
14 – 5 = 9	
15 – 5 = 10	
16 – 5 = 11	
17 – 5 = 12	

1. (a) 8 – 5 = ☐

(b) 7 – 5 = ☐

(c) 6 – 5 = ☐

(d) 5 – ☐ = ☐

2. (a) 8 – 5 = ☐   (c) 6 – 5 = ☐

(b) 7 – 5 = ☐   (d) 5 – 5 = ☐

3. (a) 6 – 5   (b) 5 – 5   (c) 8 – 5

11

Day 2 Say the tables.

Learn these:

5 – 5 = 0	
6 – 5 = 1	
7 – 5 = 2	
8 – 5 = 3	
9 – 5 = 4	9 – 5 = 4
10 – 5 = 5	10 – 5 = 5
11 – 5 = 6	11 – 5 = 6
12 – 5 = 7	
13 – 5 = 8	
14 – 5 = 9	
15 – 5 = 10	
16 – 5 = 11	
17 – 5 = 12	

1. (a) 11 – 5 = ☐

(b) 10 – 5 = ☐

(c) 9 – 5 = ☐

(d) ☐ – ☐ = ☐

2. (a) 5 + ☐ = 9, so 9 – 5 = ☐

(b) 5 + ☐ = 11, so 11 – 5 = ☐

(c) 5 + ☐ = 10, so 10 – 5 = ☐

(d) 5 + ☐ = 8, so 8 – 5 = ☐

3.

(a)	(b)	(c)	(d)
11	8	10	7
– 5	– 5	– 5	– 5
☐	☐	☐	☐

4. 9 – ☐ = 4

13

Day 3   Say the tables.

Learn these:

5 – 5 = 0			
6 – 5 = 1			
7 – 5 = 2			
8 – 5 = 3			
9 – 5 = 4			
10 – 5 = 5			
11 – 5 = 6			
12 – 5 = 7	12 – 5 = 7		
13 – 5 = 8	13 – 5 = 8		
14 – 5 = 9	14 – 5 = 9		
15 – 5 = 10			
16 – 5 = 11			
17 – 5 = 12			

1. Match.

(a) 13 – 5 •

(b) 11 – 5 •

(c) 9 – 5 •

(d) 6 – 5 •

(e) 14 – 5 •

(f) 12 – 5 •

4
1
8
7
9
6

2.

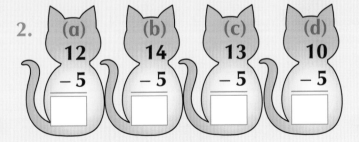

(a) 12 – 5 ▢

(b) 14 – 5 ▢

(c) 13 – 5 ▢

(d) 10 – 5 ▢

3. Complete. (Subtract.)

(a) | 12 | – | 5 | = | ▢ |

(b) | 13 | | 5 | | 8 |

(c) | 14 | | 5 | | ▢ |

(d) | 9 | | | | 4 |

▢
14

Day 4   Say the tables.

Learn these:

5 – 5 = 0			
6 – 5 = 1			
7 – 5 = 2			
8 – 5 = 3			
9 – 5 = 4			
10 – 5 = 5			
11 – 5 = 6			
12 – 5 = 7			
13 – 5 = 8			
14 – 5 = 9			
15 – 5 = 10	15 – 5 = 10		
16 – 5 = 11	16 – 5 = 11		
17 – 5 = 12	17 – 5 = 12		

1. (a) 17 – 5 = ▢

(b) 15 – 5 = ▢

(c) 16 – 5 = ▢

2.

	(a)	(b)	(c)	(d)
	16	17	15	14
	– 5	– 5	– 5	– 5
	▢	▢	▢	▢

3. Complete.

(a)   (b)

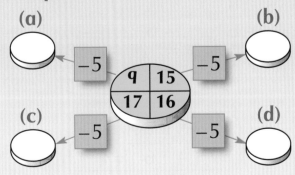

| 9 | 15 |
| 17 | 16 |

(c)   (d)

4. 16 – 5 = ▢

▢
12

Do Test 17 on page 70.

43

Subtract 6

Day 1   Say the tables.

			Learn these:
6 – 6 = 0			6 – 6 = 0
7 – 6 = 1			7 – 6 = 1
8 – 6 = 2			8 – 6 = 2
9 – 6 = 3			9 – 6 = 3
10 – 6 = 4			
11 – 6 = 5			
12 – 6 = 6			
13 – 6 = 7			
14 – 6 = 8			
15 – 6 = 9			
16 – 6 = 10			
17 – 6 = 11			
18 – 6 = 12			

1. (a) $8 - 6 = \boxed{}$

 (b) $9 - 6 = \boxed{}$

 (c) $7 - \boxed{} = \boxed{}$

2. (a) $6 - 6 = \boxed{}$ (b) $8 - 6 = \boxed{}$

 (c) $9 - 6 = \boxed{}$ (d) $7 - 6 = \boxed{}$

3.

(a)	(b)	(c)	(d)
8	6	9	7
– 6	– 6	– 6	– 6
$\boxed{}$	$\boxed{}$	$\boxed{}$	$\boxed{}$

4. Complete. (Subtract.)

 (a) $\boxed{7} - \boxed{6} = \boxed{}$

 (b) $\boxed{9}\ \boxed{}\ \boxed{6}\ \boxed{}\ \boxed{3}$

 (c) $\boxed{8}\ -\ \boxed{}\ \boxed{}\ \boxed{2}$

14

Day 2   Say the tables.

			Learn these:
6 – 6 = 0			
7 – 6 = 1			
8 – 6 = 2			
9 – 6 = 3			
10 – 6 = 4			10 – 6 = 4
11 – 6 = 5			11 – 6 = 5
12 – 6 = 6			12 – 6 = 6
13 – 6 = 7			
14 – 6 = 8			
15 – 6 = 9			
16 – 6 = 10			
17 – 6 = 11			
18 – 6 = 12			

1. (a)

 $10 - 6 = \boxed{}$

 (b)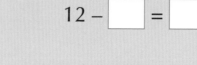

 $12 - \boxed{} = \boxed{}$

2.

(a)	(b)	(c)	(d)
10	7	12	11
– 6	– 6	– 6	– 6
$\boxed{}$	$\boxed{}$	$\boxed{}$	$\boxed{}$

3. Match.

– 6	
(a) 9•	•6
(b) 12•	•3
(c) 10•	•5
(d) 11•	•4
(e) 7•	•1

11

Day 3 Say the tables.

					Learn these:
6	–	6	=	0	
7	–	6	=	1	
8	–	6	=	2	
9	–	6	=	3	
10	–	6	=	4	
11	–	6	=	5	
12	–	6	=	6	
13	–	6	=	7	13 – 6 = 7
14	–	6	=	8	14 – 6 = 8
15	–	6	=	9	15 – 6 = 9
16	–	6	=	10	
17	–	6	=	11	
18	–	6	=	12	

1. (a)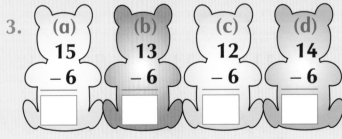

   13 – 6 = ☐

   (b)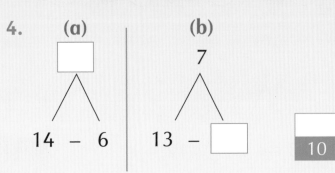

   10 – 6 = ☐

2. (a) 7 + ☐ = 13, so 13 – ☐ = 7

   (b) 9 + ☐ = 15, so 15 – ☐ = 9

3. (a) 15 – 6 ☐   (b) 13 – 6 ☐   (c) 12 – 6 ☐   (d) 14 – 6 ☐

4. (a) ☐
      / \
   14 – 6

   (b) 7
      / \
   13 – ☐

Day 4 Say the tables.

					Learn these:
6	–	6	=	0	
7	–	6	=	1	
8	–	6	=	2	
9	–	6	=	3	
10	–	6	=	4	
11	–	6	=	5	
12	–	6	=	6	
13	–	6	=	7	
14	–	6	=	8	
15	–	6	=	9	
16	–	6	=	10	16 – 6 = 10
17	–	6	=	11	17 – 6 = 11
18	–	6	=	12	18 – 6 = 12

1. (a) ●●●●●● /// /// 17 – 6 = ☐

   (b) /// 16 – ☐ = ☐

2. Complete.

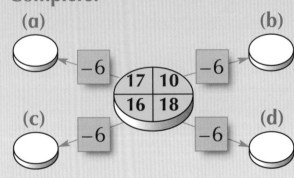

   (a)   (b)
   (c)   (d)

   –6   17 | 10   –6
        16 | 18

3. (a) 16 – 6 ☐   (b) 18 – 6 ☐   (c) 11 – 6 ☐   (d) 17 – 6 ☐

4. (a) 17 – 6 = ☐

   (b) 18 – 6 = ☐

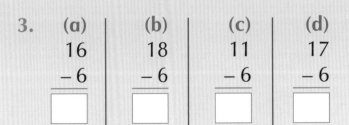

Do **Test 18** on page **70**.

45

Subtract 7

Day 1   Say the tables.

	Learn these:
7 – 7 = 0	7 – 7 = 0
8 – 7 = 1	8 – 7 = 1
9 – 7 = 2	9 – 7 = 2
10 – 7 = 3	10 – 7 = 3
11 – 7 = 4	
12 – 7 = 5	
13 – 7 = 6	
14 – 7 = 7	
15 – 7 = 8	
16 – 7 = 9	
17 – 7 = 10	
18 – 7 = 11	
19 – 7 = 12	

1. (a)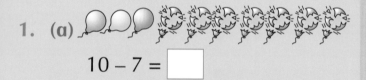

   10 – 7 = ☐

   (b)

   8 – 7 = ☐

   (c)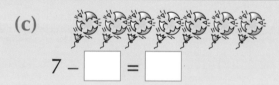

   7 – ☐ = ☐

2. (a) 7 + ☐ = 10, so 10 – 7 = ☐

   (b) 7 + ☐ = 8, so 8 – 7 = ☐

   (c) 7 + ☐ = 9, so 9 – 7 = ☐

   (d) 7 + ☐ = 7, so 7 – 7 = ☐

3.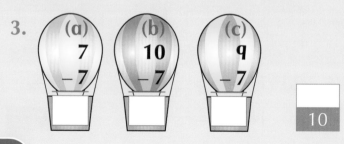

   (a) 7 – 7 = ☐   (b) 10 – 7 = ☐   (c) 9 – 7 = ☐

   10

Day 2   Say the tables.

	Learn these:
7 – 7 = 0	
8 – 7 = 1	
9 – 7 = 2	
10 – 7 = 3	
11 – 7 = 4	11 – 7 = 4
12 – 7 = 5	12 – 7 = 5
13 – 7 = 6	13 – 7 = 6
14 – 7 = 7	
15 – 7 = 8	
16 – 7 = 9	
17 – 7 = 10	
18 – 7 = 11	
19 – 7 = 12	

1. (a)

   11 – 7 = ☐

   (b)

   13 – 7 = ☐

   (c)

   12 – 7 = ☐

2.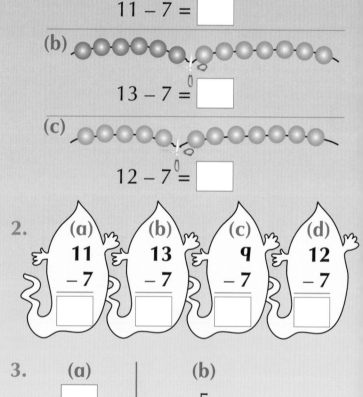

   (a) 11 – 7 = ☐   (b) 13 – 7 = ☐   (c) 9 – 7 = ☐   (d) 12 – 7 = ☐

3. (a) ☐
   13 – 7

   (b) 5
   12 – ☐

   9

Day 3 Say the tables.

Learn these:

7 – 7 = 0
8 – 7 = 1
9 – 7 = 2
10 – 7 = 3
11 – 7 = 4
12 – 7 = 5
13 – 7 = 6
14 – 7 = 7   14 – 7 = 7
15 – 7 = 8   15 – 7 = 8
16 – 7 = 9   16 – 7 = 9
17 – 7 = 10
18 – 7 = 11
19 – 7 = 12

1. (a) ▦ 14 – 7 = ☐

   (b) ▦ 16 – ☐ = 9

2. Match.

   (a) 14 – 7 •   6
   (b) 16 – 7 •   7
   (c) 13 – 7 •   5
   (d) 12 – 7 •   9

3. (a)   (b)   (c)   (d)
   15   14   16   13
   – 7   – 7   – 7   – 7
   ☐   ☐   ☐   ☐

4. (a) 16 – ☐ = 9
   (b) 14 – ☐ = 7
   (c) 15 – ☐ = 8   ☐
                                    13

Day 4 Say the tables.

Learn these:

7 – 7 = 0
8 – 7 = 1
9 – 7 = 2
10 – 7 = 3
11 – 7 = 4
12 – 7 = 5
13 – 7 = 6
14 – 7 = 7
15 – 7 = 8
16 – 7 = 9
17 – 7 = 10   17 – 7 = 10
18 – 7 = 11   18 – 7 = 11
19 – 7 = 12   19 – 7 = 12

1. Complete.

   (a)   (b)

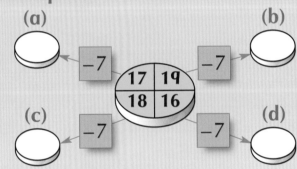

   (c)   (d)

2. (a) 🍵18 – 🍵7 = ☐
   (b) 🍵17 – 🍵7 = ☐
   (c) 🍵19 – 🍵7 = ☐

3. (a)   (b)   (c)   (d)
   17   19   18   12
   – 7   – 7   – 7   – 7
   ☐   ☐   ☐   ☐

4. (a) 18 – ☐ = 11
   (b) 17 – 7 = ☐   ☐
                                    13

Do **Test 19** on page **71**.

47

Subtract 8

Day 1   Say the tables.

	Learn these:
8 – 8 = 0	8 – 8 = 0
9 – 8 = 1	9 – 8 = 1
10 – 8 = 2	10 – 8 = 2
11 – 8 = 3	11 – 8 = 3
12 – 8 = 4	
13 – 8 = 5	
14 – 8 = 6	
15 – 8 = 7	
16 – 8 = 8	
17 – 8 = 9	
18 – 8 = 10	
19 – 8 = 11	
20 – 8 = 12	

1. (a) $10 - 8 = \boxed{}$

(b) $11 - 8 = \boxed{}$

2. (a) $10 - 8 = \boxed{}$ (c) $8 - 8 = \boxed{}$

(b) $11 - 8 = \boxed{}$ (d) $9 - 8 = \boxed{}$

3.

(a) 9 − 8 = ☐   (b) 8 − 8 = ☐   (c) 10 − 8 = ☐   (d) 11 − 8 = ☐

4. Match.

(a) 11 – 8 •   1

(b) 9 – 8 •   3

(c) 8 – 8 •   2

(d) 10 – 8 •   0   14

Day 2   Say the tables.

	Learn these:
8 – 8 = 0	
9 – 8 = 1	
10 – 8 = 2	
11 – 8 = 3	
12 – 8 = 4	12 – 8 = 4
13 – 8 = 5	13 – 8 = 5
14 – 8 = 6	14 – 8 = 6
15 – 8 = 7	
16 – 8 = 8	
17 – 8 = 9	
18 – 8 = 10	
19 – 8 = 11	
20 – 8 = 12	

1. Count back 8.

(a) ☐ 12   (b) ☐ 14

(c) ☐ 13   (d) ☐ 11

2.

(a)	(b)	(c)	(d)
13	11	9	14
− 8	− 8	− 8	− 8
☐	☐	☐	☐

3.

	− 8			− 8
(a)	13	(d)	10	
(b)	12	(e)	14	
(c)	8	(f)	11	

4. (a) $12 - \boxed{} = 4$

(b) $14 - \boxed{} = 6$

(c) $13 - \boxed{} = 5$ 17

Day 3 — Say the tables.

Learn these:

8 – 8 = 0
9 – 8 = 1
10 – 8 = 2
11 – 8 = 3
12 – 8 = 4
13 – 8 = 5
14 – 8 = 6
15 – 8 = 7   15 – 8 = 7
16 – 8 = 8   16 – 8 = 8
17 – 8 = 9   17 – 8 = 9
18 – 8 = 10
19 – 8 = 11
20 – 8 = 12

1. (a) 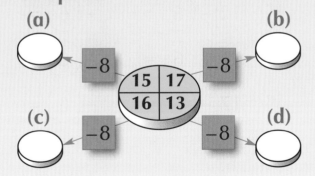 16 – 8 = ☐

(b) 17 – 8 = ☐

2. Complete.

(a)   (b)

–8 | 15 | 17 | –8
      | 16 | 13 |

(c)   –8   –8   (d)

3. (a) 9 – 8 = ☐   (c) 17 – 8 = ☐

(b) 15 – 8 = ☐   (d) 16 – 8 = ☐

4. Complete. (Subtract.)

(a) | 16 | – | 8 | = | ☐ |

(b) | 15 | | 8 | | 7 | ☐

12

Day 4 — Say the tables.

Learn these:

8 – 8 = 0
9 – 8 = 1
10 – 8 = 2
11 – 8 = 3
12 – 8 = 4
13 – 8 = 5
14 – 8 = 6
15 – 8 = 7
16 – 8 = 8
17 – 8 = 9
18 – 8 = 10   18 – 8 = 10
19 – 8 = 11   19 – 8 = 11
20 – 8 = 12   20 – 8 = 12

1. (a) 20 – 8 = ☐

(b) 18 – 8 = ☐

(c) 19 – 8 = ☐

2.
(a)	(b)	(c)	(d)
19	14	18	20
– 8	– 8	– 8	– 8
☐	☐	☐	☐

3. (a) 20 – 8 = ☐

(b) 18 – 8 = ☐

(c) 19 – 8 = ☐

(d) 16 – 8 = ☐

(e) 11 – 8 = ☐   ☐

12

Do Test 20 on page 71.

49

Revision E. Subtraction (– 5) to (– 8)

Revision 17

1. (a)

   8 – 5 = ☐

   (b)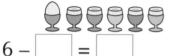

   6 – ☐ = ☐

   (c)

   ☐ – ☐ = ☐

2. (a) – = ☐

   (b) – = ☐

   (c) – = ☐

   (d) – = ☐

3.
(a)	(b)	(c)	(d)
9	5	14	12
– 5	– 5	– 5	– 5
☐	☐	☐	☐

4. Complete.

   (a)   (b)   (c)   (d)

   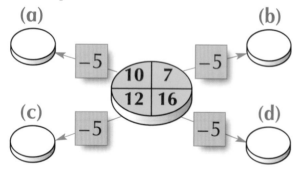

5. Match.

   (a) 5 – 5

   (b) 15 – 5 •

   (c) 17 – 5 •

   (d) 12 – 5 •

   (e) 6 – 5 •

   | 1 |
   | 12 |
   | 0 |
   | 10 |
   | 7 |

   20

Revision 18

1.
(a)	(b)	(c)	(d)
8	6	10	12
– 6	– 6	– 6	– 6
☐	☐	☐	☐

2. Ring the correct answer.

   (a) 9 – 6 = | 4 | 3 | 2 |

   (b) 11 – 6 = | 5 | 6 | 8 |

   (c) 14 – 6 = | 8 | 7 | 9 |

   (d) 12 – 6 = | 9 | 10 | 6 |

   (e) 16 – 6 = | 14 | 12 | 10 |

   (f) 18 – 6 = | 12 | 10 | 14 |

3. Fill in the gaps.

   (a) ☐8 – ⭕6 ⇒ ☐2 – ⭕1 = ☐1

   (b) ☐10 – ⭕6 ⇒ ☐ – ⭕2 = ☐

   (c) ☐12 – ⭕6 ⇒ ☐ – ⭕6 = ☐

   (d) ☐14 – ⭕6 ⇒ ☐ – ⭕6 = ☐

   (e) ☐17 – ⭕6 ⇒ ☐ – ⭕6 = ☐

4. Match.

– 6	
(a) 7•	•9
(b) 9•	•4
(c) 12•	•1
(d) 15•	•3
(e) 10•	•6

   20

Revision 19

1. (a)

   $q - 7 = \boxed{}$

   (b)

   $12 - 7 = \boxed{}$

   (c)

   $14 - 7 = \boxed{}$

2.
(a)	(b)	(c)	(d)
8	10	13	15
− 7	− 7	− 7	− 7
$\boxed{}$	$\boxed{}$	$\boxed{}$	$\boxed{}$

3. Count back 7.

   (a) $\boxed{}\ \boxed{q}$ (b) $\boxed{}\ \boxed{12}$

   (c) $\boxed{}\ \boxed{15}$ (d) $\boxed{}\ \boxed{14}$

4. (a) $10 - 7 = \boxed{}$ (b) $7 - 7 = \boxed{}$

   (c) $12 - 7 = \boxed{}$ (d) $16 - 7 = \boxed{}$

5. (a) (b) $\boxed{6}$ (c)

   $\boxed{}$

   $10 - 7$ | $13 - \boxed{}$ | $16 - 7$

6. Complete. (Subtract.)

   (a) | 8 | − | 7 | = | |

   (b) | 10 | | 7 | | 3 |

   20

Revision 20

1. (a)

   $11 - 8 = \boxed{}$

   (b)

   $q - \boxed{} = \boxed{}$

   (c)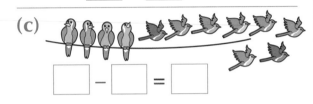

   $\boxed{} - \boxed{} = \boxed{}$

2.
	− 8	
(a)	q	
(b)	12	
(c)	14	

	− 8	
(d)	8	
(e)	16	
(f)	18	

3.
(a)	(b)	(c)	(d)
12	10	16	18
− 8	− 8	− 8	− 8
$\boxed{}$	$\boxed{}$	$\boxed{}$	$\boxed{}$

4. Fill in the gaps.

   (a) $\boxed{10} - \bigcirc{8} \Rightarrow \boxed{2} - \bigcirc{1} = \boxed{}$

   (b) $\boxed{13} - \bigcirc{8} \Rightarrow \boxed{} - \bigcirc{3} = \boxed{}$

   (c) $\boxed{16} - \bigcirc{8} \Rightarrow \boxed{} - \bigcirc{8} = \boxed{}$

   (d) $\boxed{17} - \bigcirc{8} \Rightarrow \boxed{} - \bigcirc{8} = \boxed{}$

   (e) $\boxed{20} - \bigcirc{8} \Rightarrow \boxed{} - \bigcirc{8} = \boxed{}$

5. (a) $12 - \boxed{} = 4$

   (b) $18 - 8 = \boxed{}$

   20

Record your **scores** on page **77**.

Subtract 9

Day 1 — Say the tables.

9 – 9 =	0		
10 – 9 =	1		
11 – 9 =	2		
12 – 9 =	3		
13 – 9 =	4		
14 – 9 =	5		
15 – 9 =	6		
16 – 9 =	7		
17 – 9 =	8		
18 – 9 =	9		
19 – 9 =	10		
20 – 9 =	11		
21 – 9 =	12		

Learn these:

9 – 9 = 0
10 – 9 = 1
11 – 9 = 2
12 – 9 = 3

Day 2 — Say the tables.

9 – 9 =	0
10 – 9 =	1
11 – 9 =	2
12 – 9 =	3
13 – 9 =	4
14 – 9 =	5
15 – 9 =	6
16 – 9 =	7
17 – 9 =	8
18 – 9 =	9
19 – 9 =	10
20 – 9 =	11
21 – 9 =	12

Learn these:

13 – 9 = 4
14 – 9 = 5
15 – 9 = 6

Day 1

1. (a)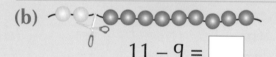

12 – 9 = ☐

(b) 11 – 9 = ☐

(c) 10 – 9 = ☐

(d) 9 – 9 = ☐

2.

(a)	(b)	(c)	(d)
9	12	11	10
– 9	– 9	– 9	– 9
☐	☐	☐	☐

3. Match.

(a) 9 – 9 •   3

(b) 12 – 9 •   2

(c) 11 – 9 •   0   11

Day 2

1. (a)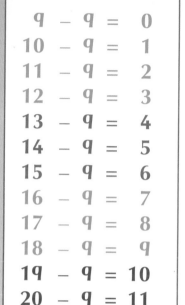

13 – 9 = ☐

(b) 15 – 9 = ☐

(c) 14 – 9 = ☐

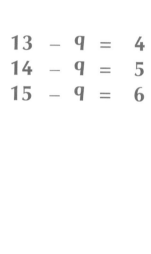

2.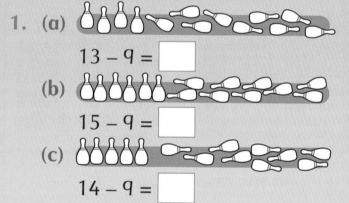

(a) 15 – 9 ☐   (b) 13 – 9 ☐   (c) 14 – 9 ☐   (d) 12 – 9 ☐

3. (a) 13 – 9 = ☐

(b) 15 – ☐ = 6

4. Fill in the gaps.

(a) 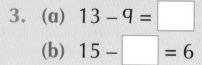 14 → –9 → 5 → –4 → ☐

(b)  15 → –9 → ☐ → –3 → ☐   11

Day 3 — Say the tables.

Learn these:

$9 - 9 = 0$
$10 - 9 = 1$
$11 - 9 = 2$
$12 - 9 = 3$
$13 - 9 = 4$
$14 - 9 = 5$
$15 - 9 = 6$
$16 - 9 = 7$ $16 - 9 = 7$
$17 - 9 = 8$ $17 - 9 = 8$
$18 - 9 = 9$ $18 - 9 = 9$
$19 - 9 = 10$
$20 - 9 = 11$
$21 - 9 = 12$

1. (a) $16 - 9 = \boxed{}$

   (b) $17 - 9 = \boxed{}$

   (c) $18 - 9 = \boxed{}$

2. (a)
   9
   $18 - \boxed{}$

   (b)
   $\boxed{}$
   $17 - 9$

   (c)
   7
   $16 - \boxed{}$

3. Match.

   (a) $17 - 9$ 7

   (b) $18 - 9$ 9

   (c) $16 - 9$ 8

   (d) $14 - 9$ 5

   (e) $15 - 9$ 6   11

Day 4 — Say the tables.

Learn these:

$9 - 9 = 0$
$10 - 9 = 1$
$11 - 9 = 2$
$12 - 9 = 3$
$13 - 9 = 4$
$14 - 9 = 5$
$15 - 9 = 6$
$16 - 9 = 7$
$17 - 9 = 8$
$18 - 9 = 9$
$19 - 9 = 10$ $19 - 9 = 10$
$20 - 9 = 11$ $20 - 9 = 11$
$21 - 9 = 12$ $21 - 9 = 12$

1.
   (a) $20 - 9$ $\boxed{}$
   (b) $18 - 9$ $\boxed{}$
   (c) $21 - 9$ $\boxed{}$
   (d) $19 - 9$ $\boxed{}$

2. Fill in the gaps.

   (a) $\boxed{10} - \bigcirc{9} \Rightarrow \boxed{1} + \bigcirc{3} = \boxed{}$

   (b) $\boxed{12} - \bigcirc{9} \Rightarrow \boxed{} - \bigcirc{1} = \boxed{}$

   (c) $\boxed{19} - \bigcirc{9} \Rightarrow \boxed{} - \bigcirc{9} = \boxed{}$

   (d) $\boxed{21} - \bigcirc{9} \Rightarrow \boxed{} - \bigcirc{9} = \boxed{}$

   (e) $\boxed{20} - \bigcirc{9} \Rightarrow \boxed{} - \bigcirc{9} = \boxed{}$

3. (a) $19 - 9 = \boxed{}$

   (b) $21 - 9 = \boxed{}$

   (c) $20 - 9 = \boxed{}$

   (d) $17 - 9 = \boxed{}$ 13

Do Test 21 on page 72.

Subtract 10

Day 1 — Say the tables.

	Learn these:
10 – 10 = 0	10 – 10 = 0
11 – 10 = 1	11 – 10 = 1
12 – 10 = 2	12 – 10 = 2
13 – 10 = 3	13 – 10 = 3
14 – 10 = 4	
15 – 10 = 5	
16 – 10 = 6	
17 – 10 = 7	
18 – 10 = 8	
19 – 10 = 9	
20 – 10 = 10	
21 – 10 = 11	
22 – 10 = 12	

Day 2 — Say the tables.

	Learn these:
10 – 10 = 0	
11 – 10 = 1	
12 – 10 = 2	
13 – 10 = 3	
14 – 10 = 4	14 – 10 = 4
15 – 10 = 5	15 – 10 = 5
16 – 10 = 6	16 – 10 = 6
17 – 10 = 7	
18 – 10 = 8	
19 – 10 = 9	
20 – 10 = 10	
21 – 10 = 11	
22 – 10 = 12	

Day 1

1. (a)

13 – 10 = ▢

(b) 11 – 10 = ▢

(c) 12 – ▢ = ▢

2.

(a) 11 – 10 ▢
(b) 10 – 10 ▢
(c) 13 – 10 ▢
(d) 12 – 10 ▢

3. Match.

(a) 13 – 10 •
(b) 10 – 10 •
(c) 12 – 10 •
(d) 11 – 10 •

1
3
0
2
11

Day 2

1. (a) 15 – 10 = ▢

(b) 14 – 10 = ▢

(c) 16 – ▢ = ▢

2.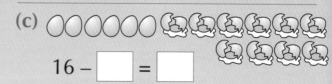

	– 10
(a)	16
(b)	14
(c)	10

	– 10
(d)	12
(e)	15
(f)	11

3.

(a)	(b)	(c)
15	16	14
– 10	– 10	– 10
▢	▢	▢

12

Day 3   Say the tables.

Learn these:

$$10 - 10 = 0$$
$$11 - 10 = 1$$
$$12 - 10 = 2$$
$$13 - 10 = 3$$
$$14 - 10 = 4$$
$$15 - 10 = 5$$
$$16 - 10 = 6$$
$$17 - 10 = 7$$
$$18 - 10 = 8$$
$$19 - 10 = 9$$
$$20 - 10 = 10$$
$$21 - 10 = 11$$
$$22 - 10 = 12$$

Learn these:
$$17 - 10 = 7$$
$$18 - 10 = 8$$
$$19 - 10 = 9$$

1. (a) $18 - 10 = \boxed{}$

   (b) $19 - 10 = \boxed{}$

   (b) $17 - 10 = \boxed{}$

2.
(a)	(b)	(c)	(d)
17	13	18	19
− 10	− 10	− 10	− 10
$\boxed{}$	$\boxed{}$	$\boxed{}$	$\boxed{}$

3. (a) $17 - 10 = \boxed{}$

   (b) $15 - 10 = \boxed{}$

   (c) $18 - 10 = \boxed{}$

   (d) $19 - 10 = \boxed{}$

11

Day 4   Say the tables.

Learn these:

$$10 - 10 = 0$$
$$11 - 10 = 1$$
$$12 - 10 = 2$$
$$13 - 10 = 3$$
$$14 - 10 = 4$$
$$15 - 10 = 5$$
$$16 - 10 = 6$$
$$17 - 10 = 7$$
$$18 - 10 = 8$$
$$19 - 10 = 9$$
$$20 - 10 = 10$$
$$21 - 10 = 11$$
$$22 - 10 = 12$$

Learn these:
$$20 - 10 = 10$$
$$21 - 10 = 11$$
$$22 - 10 = 12$$

1. Complete.

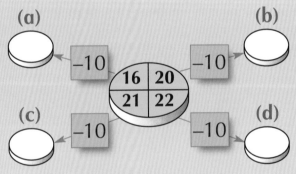

2.
(a)	(b)	(c)	(d)
21	20	15	22
− 10	− 10	− 10	− 10
$\boxed{}$	$\boxed{}$	$\boxed{}$	$\boxed{}$

3. ✔ or ✗

   (a) $21 - 10 = 10$ $\boxed{}$

   (b) $14 - 10 = 4$ $\boxed{}$

   (c) $19 - 10 = 9$ $\boxed{}$

   (d) $22 - 10 = 12$ $\boxed{}$

12

Do **Test 22** on page **72**.

55

Subtract 11

Day 1 — Say the tables.

| 11 – 11 = 0 |
| 12 – 11 = 1 |
| 13 – 11 = 2 |
| 14 – 11 = 3 |
| 15 – 11 = 4 |
| 16 – 11 = 5 |
| 17 – 11 = 6 |
| 18 – 11 = 7 |
| 19 – 11 = 8 |
| 20 – 11 = 9 |
| 21 – 11 = 10 |
| 22 – 11 = 11 |
| 23 – 11 = 12 |

Learn these:

11 – 11 = 0
12 – 11 = 1
13 – 11 = 2
14 – 11 = 3

Day 2 — Say the tables.

| 11 – 11 = 0 |
| 12 – 11 = 1 |
| 13 – 11 = 2 |
| 14 – 11 = 3 |
| 15 – 11 = 4 |
| 16 – 11 = 5 |
| 17 – 11 = 6 |
| 18 – 11 = 7 |
| 19 – 11 = 8 |
| 20 – 11 = 9 |
| 21 – 11 = 10 |
| 22 – 11 = 11 |
| 23 – 11 = 12 |

Learn these:

15 – 11 = 4
16 – 11 = 5
17 – 11 = 6

Day 1

1. (a)  14 – 11 = ☐

(b)  13 – 11 = ☐

(c) 12 – ☐ = 1

(d) 11 – ☐ = ☐

2.
(a)	(b)	(c)	(d)
13	14	12	11
– 11	– 11	– 11	– 11
☐	☐	☐	☐

3. (a) 13 – 11 = ☐

(b) 14 – 11 = ☐

(c) 12 – 11 = ☐

(d) 11 – 11 = ☐

12

Day 2

1. (a) 16 – 11 = ☐

(b) 15 – ☐ = ☐

(c) 17 – ☐ = ☐

2. (a) 11 + ☐ = 17, so 17 – 11 = ☐

(b) 11 + ☐ = 15, so 15 – 11 = ☐

(c) 11 + ☐ = 16, so 16 – 11 = ☐

3.
(a)	(b)	(c)	(d)
17	14	15	16
– 11	– 11	– 11	– 11
☐	☐	☐	☐

4. (a) 16 – 11 = ☐

(b) 17 – ☐ = 6

(c) 15 – 11 = ☐

(d) 14 – ☐ = 3

14

Day 3   Say the tables.

Learn these:

11	– 11	=	0
12	– 11	=	1
13	– 11	=	2
14	– 11	=	3
15	– 11	=	4
16	– 11	=	5
17	– 11	=	6
18	– 11	=	7
19	– 11	=	8
20	– 11	=	9
21	– 11	=	10
22	– 11	=	11
23	– 11	=	12

Learn these:

18 – 11 = 7
19 – 11 = 8
20 – 11 = 9

Day 4   Say the tables.

Learn these:

11	– 11	=	0
12	– 11	=	1
13	– 11	=	2
14	– 11	=	3
15	– 11	=	4
16	– 11	=	5
17	– 11	=	6
18	– 11	=	7
19	– 11	=	8
20	– 11	=	9
21	– 11	=	10
22	– 11	=	11
23	– 11	=	12

Learn these:

21 – 11 = 10
22 – 11 = 11
23 – 11 = 12

Day 3

1. (a) 21 – 11 = ☐

   (b) 20 – ☐ = ☐

2. (a) 16 – 11 ☐   (b) 18 – 11 ☐   (c) 20 – 11 ☐   (d) 19 – 11 ☐

3. Match.

   (a) 15 – 11 •   7
   (b) 18 – 11 •   9
   (c) 14 – 11 •   2
   (d) 20 – 11 •   4
   (e) 19 – 11 •   3
   (f) 13 – 11 •   8   12

Day 4

1.
(a)	(b)	(c)	(d)
21	17	23	22
– 11	– 11	– 11	– 11
☐	☐	☐	☐

2. Fill in the gaps.

   (a) 12 – 11 ⇒ 1 + 3 = ☐

   (b) 22 – 11 ⇒ ☐ – 1 = ☐

   (c) 19 – 11 ⇒ ☐ + 4 = ☐

   (d) 21 – 11 ⇒ ☐ – 3 = ☐

   (e) 23 – 11 ⇒ ☐ – 11 = ☐

3. (a) 22 – 11 = ☐

   (b) 21 – 11 = ☐

   (c) 23 – 11 = ☐   12

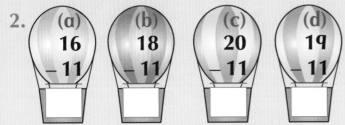

Do **Test 23** on page **73**.

Subtract 12

Day 1 — Say the tables.

	Learn these:
12 – 12 = 0	12 – 12 = 0
13 – 12 = 1	13 – 12 = 1
14 – 12 = 2	14 – 12 = 2
15 – 12 = 3	15 – 12 = 3
16 – 12 = 4	
17 – 12 = 5	
18 – 12 = 6	
19 – 12 = 7	
20 – 12 = 8	
21 – 12 = 9	
22 – 12 = 10	
23 – 12 = 11	
24 – 12 = 12	

Day 2 — Say the tables.

	Learn these:
12 – 12 = 0	
13 – 12 = 1	
14 – 12 = 2	
15 – 12 = 3	
16 – 12 = 4	16 – 12 = 4
17 – 12 = 5	17 – 12 = 5
18 – 12 = 6	18 – 12 = 6
19 – 12 = 7	
20 – 12 = 8	
21 – 12 = 9	
22 – 12 = 10	
23 – 12 = 11	
24 – 12 = 12	

Day 1

1. (a) 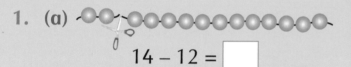 14 – 12 = ☐

(b) 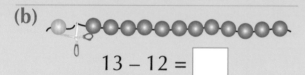 13 – 12 = ☐

(c) 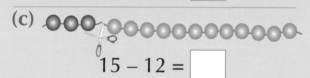 15 – 12 = ☐

2.
(a)	(b)	(c)	(d)
12	13	15	14
– 12	– 12	– 12	– 12
☐	☐	☐	☐

3.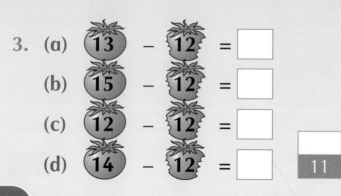
(a) 13 – 12 = ☐
(b) 15 – 12 = ☐
(c) 12 – 12 = ☐
(d) 14 – 12 = ☐   11

Day 2

1. (a)  17 – 12 = ☐

(b) 18 – 12 = ☐

(c) 16 – ☐ = ☐

2.
(a)	(b)	(c)
6	☐	5
18 – ☐	16 – 12	17 – ☐

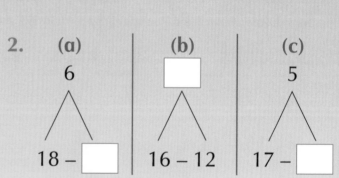

3.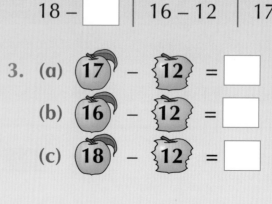
(a) 17 – 12 = ☐
(b) 16 – 12 = ☐
(c) 18 – 12 = ☐   9

Day 3 Say the tables.

Learn these:

12	− 12	=	0
13	− 12	=	1
14	− 12	=	2
15	− 12	=	3
16	− 12	=	4
17	− 12	=	5
18	− 12	=	6
19	− 12	=	7
20	− 12	=	8
21	− 12	=	9
22	− 12	=	10
23	− 12	=	11
24	− 12	=	12

Learn these:
19 − 12 = 7
20 − 12 = 8
21 − 12 = 9

1. (a)  21 − 12 = ☐

   (b) 20 − 12 = ☐

   (c) 19 − 12 = ☐

2. **Ring the correct answer.**

   (a) 20 − 12 =   7 8 9

   (b) 18 − 12 =   5 6 7

   (c) 21 − 12 =   7 8 9

3. ✔ or ✗

   (a) 21 − 12 = 10   ☐

   (b) 17 − 12 = 6   ☐

   (c) 18 − 12 = 6   ☐

   (d) 21 − 12 = 9   ☐   10

Day 4 Say the tables.

Learn these:

12	− 12	=	0
13	− 12	=	1
14	− 12	=	2
15	− 12	=	3
16	− 12	=	4
17	− 12	=	5
18	− 12	=	6
19	− 12	=	7
20	− 12	=	8
21	− 12	=	9
22	− 12	=	10
23	− 12	=	11
24	− 12	=	12

Learn these:
22 − 12 = 10
23 − 12 = 11
24 − 12 = 12

1. **Complete.**

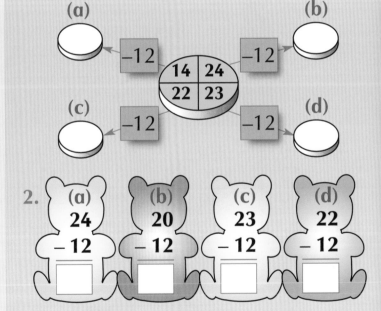

(a)   (b)   (c)   (d)

−12   14 24
        22 23

2. (a) 24 − 12 = ☐
   (b) 20 − 12 = ☐
   (c) 23 − 12 = ☐
   (d) 22 − 12 = ☐

3. **Complete. (Subtract.)**

   (a) 13 − 12 = ☐

   (b) 23 ☐ 12 = 11

   (c) 17 − ☐ = 5

   (d) 24 ☐ 12 ☐ 12

   (e) 22 − ☐ ☐ 10   13

 Do **Test 24** on page **73**.

Revision F   Subtraction (– 9) to (– 12)

Revision 21

1. (a)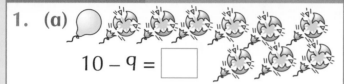

10 – 9 = ☐

(b)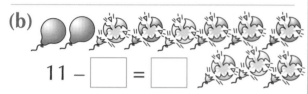

11 – ☐ = ☐

2.

(a)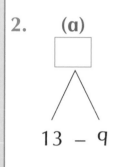

☐

13 – 9

(b)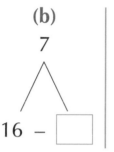

7

16 – ☐

(c)

☐

14 – 9

3. (a) ⑭ – 🥚9 = ☐

(b) ⑯ – 🥚9 = ☐

(c) ⑰ – 🥚9 = ☐

(d) ⑲ – 🥚9 = ☐

(e) ⑫ – 🥚9 = ☐

4.

(a)	(b)	(c)	(d)
13	20	9	11
– 9	– 9	– 9	– 9
☐	☐	☐	☐

5. Match.

(a) 10 – 9 •   ☐ 2

(b) 20 – 9 •   ☐ 9

(c) 18 – 9 •   ☐ 8

(d) 11 – 9 •   ☐ 0

(e) 9 – 9 •   ☐ 1

(f) 17 – 9 •   ☐ 11

☐

20

Revision 22

1. (a)

13 – 10 = ☐

(b)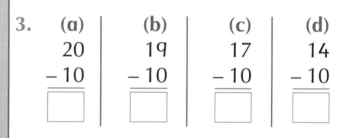

☐ – ☐ = ☐

2. Complete.

(a)   (b)

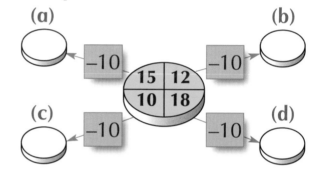

(c)   (d)

3.

(a)	(b)	(c)	(d)
20	19	17	14
– 10	– 10	– 10	– 10
☐	☐	☐	☐

4.

– 10	
(a) 14	
(b) 11	
(c) 18	

– 10	
(d) 17	
(e) 20	
(f) 22	

5. (a) ⑪ – ⑩ = ☐

(b) ⑮ – ⑩ = ☐

(c) ⑰ – ⑩ = ☐

(d) ⑳ – ⑩ = ☐

☐

20

Revision 23

1. (a)

$15 - 11 = \boxed{}$

(b)

$14 - \boxed{} = \boxed{}$

(c)

$17 - \boxed{} = \boxed{}$

2.
(a)	(b)	(c)	(d)
14	16	11	17
− 11	− 11	− 11	− 11
$\boxed{}$	$\boxed{}$	$\boxed{}$	$\boxed{}$

3. Match.

(a) 12 − 11   7
(b) 20 − 11   4
(c) 13 − 11   8
(d) 19 − 11   1
(e) 15 − 11   9
(f) 18 − 11   2

4. (a) 15 − 11 = $\boxed{}$

(b) 11 − 11 = $\boxed{}$

5. Complete. (Subtract.)

(a) | 14 | − | 11 | = | | |
(b) | 16 | | 11 | = | 5 |
(c) | 17 | − | | = | 6 |
(d) | 23 | | | = | 12 |
(e) | 21 | − | 11 | | |

20

Revision 24

1. (a)

$16 - 12 = \boxed{}$

(b)

$14 - \boxed{} = \boxed{}$

(c)

$\boxed{} - \boxed{} = \boxed{}$

(d)

$13 - \boxed{} = \boxed{}$

2.
(a)	(b)	(c)	(d)
14	17	19	12
− 12	− 12	− 12	− 12
$\boxed{}$	$\boxed{}$	$\boxed{}$	$\boxed{}$

3.

	− 12	
(a)	15	
(b)	18	
(c)	12	

	− 12	
(d)	14	
(e)	20	
(f)	24	

4. Match.

(a) 13 − 12   8
(b) 20 − 12   0
(c) 24 − 12   10
(d) 22 − 12   1
(e) 17 − 12   5
(f) 12 − 12   12

20

Tests Addition (+ 1) to (+ 4)

Test 1

1. (a)
   3 + 1 = ☐

   (b)

   5 + ☐ = ☐

   (c)

   7 + ☐ = ☐

   (d)
   ☐ + ☐ = ☐

2.
(a)	(b)	(c)	(d)
4	1	8	10
+ 1	+ 1	+ 1	+ 1
☐	☐	☐	☐

3. (a) 8 + 1 = ☐
   (b) 5 + 1 = ☐

4. Match.
   (a) 2 + 1
   (b) 6 + 1
   (c) 9 + 1
   (d) 11 + 1
   (e) 7 + 1

   10
   12
   8
   7
   3

5. (a) ⑤ + ① = ☐
   (b) ⑧ + ① = ☐
   (c) ⑫ + ① = ☐
   (d) ⑨ + ① = ☐
   (e) ⑪ + ① = ☐

   20

Test 2

1. (a) ●●●●○○ 4 + 2 = ☐

   (b) ○○○○○○●● 7 + 2 = ☐

   (c) ●●●●●●●●●○○
   8 + ☐ = ☐

   (d) ○○○○○○○○○○○●○
   ☐ + ☐ = ☐

2. Complete.

   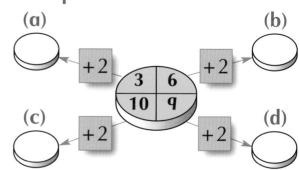
   (a)   (b)
   +2   +2
   | 3 | 6 |
   | 10 | 9 |
   (c)   (d)
   +2   +2

3. (a) ❀4 + ❀2 = ☐
   (b) ❀6 + ❀2 = ☐
   (c) ❀9 + ❀2 = ☐
   (d) ❀12 + ❀2 = ☐

4.
(a)	(b)	(c)	(d)
5	2	8	11
+ 2	+ 2	+ 2	+ 2
☐	☐	☐	☐

5. (a) 1 + ☐ = 3
   (b) 3 + 2 = ☐
   (c) 5 + ☐ = 7
   (d) 8 + 2 = ☐

   20

Test 3

1. (a) ●●●●●●● + ●●●

   7 + 3 = ☐

   (b) ●●●●● + ●●●

   5 + 3 = ☐

   (c) ●●●●●●●●●●● + ●●●

   10 + ☐ = ☐

2.

(a)	(b)	(c)	(d)
3	6	8	11
+ 3	+ 3	+ 3	+ 3
☐	☐	☐	☐

3. (a) **4** + **3** = ☐

   (b) **7** + **3** = ☐

   (c) **q** + **3** = ☐

   (d) **11** + **3** = ☐

4. Match.

   (a) 5 + 3 •   11

   (b) 6 + 3 •   8

   (c) 12 + 3 •   q

   (d) 8 + 3 •   15

5. Match.

	+ 3	
(a)	6•	•11
(b)	q•	• 4
(c)	1•	• q
(d)	7•	•12
(e)	8•	•10

   20

Test 4

1. (a) [::] + [::]   4 + 4 = ☐

   (b) [:::] + [::]   6 + 4 = ☐

   (c) [:::] + [::]

   ☐ + ☐ = ☐

2.

(a)	(b)	(c)	(d)
5	q	4	11
+ 4	+ 4	+ 4	+ 4
☐	☐	☐	☐

3. Complete.

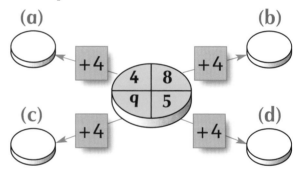

   (a)   (b)

   (c)   (d)

4. Count on 4.

   (a) | 5 | ☐ | (b) | 8 | ☐ |

   (c) | 6 | ☐ | (d) | 11 | ☐ |

5. (a) **6** + **4** = ☐

   (b) **8** + **4** = ☐

   (c) **10** + **4** = ☐

   (d) **12** + **4** = ☐

   (e) **0** + **4** = ☐   ☐

   20

Record your **scores** on page **76**.   63

Test 5

1. (a) 2 + 5 = ☐

   (b) 4 + 5 = ☐

   (c) 8 + ☐ = ☐

2. (a) 3 + 5 = ☐

   (b) 7 + 5 = ☐

   (c) 9 + 5 = ☐

   (d) 12 + 5 = ☐

3.

(a)	(b)	(c)	(d)
1	5	8	11
+ 5	+ 5	+ 5	+ 5
☐	☐	☐	☐

4. Match.

   (a) 2 + 5 •   5

   (b) 8 + 5 •   10

   (c) 0 + 5 •   7

   (d) 5 + 5 •   13

5.

+	(a) 2	(b) 5	(c) 4	(d) 7	(e) 6
5					

20

Test 6

1. (a) 3 + 6 = ☐

   (b) 5 + 6 = ☐

   (c) 8 + ☐ = ☐

2.

(a)	(b)	(c)	(d)
1	5	9	11
+ 6	+ 6	+ 6	+ 6
☐	☐	☐	☐

3. (a) 4 + 6 = ☐

   (b) 7 + 6 = ☐

   (c) 5 + 6 = ☐

   (d) 10 + 6 = ☐

4. Ring the correct answer.

   (a) 6 + 6 = | 10 | 12 | 14 |

   (b) 9 + 6 = | 15 | 16 | 17 |

   (c) 12 + 6 = | 16 | 20 | 18 |

   (d) 8 + 6 = | 15 | 14 | 13 |

5. Complete. (Add.)

   (a) | 0 | + | 6 | = | ☐ |

   (b) | 3 | | 6 | | 9 |

   (c) | 5 | | 6 | | 11 |

   (d) | 9 | | 6 | = | ☐ |

   (e) | 11 | + | ☐ | | 17 |

20

64

Test 7

1. (a) 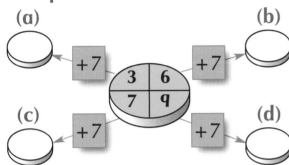 •• + •••••••

   2 + 7 = ☐

   (b) ••••• + ••••••

   5 + 7 = ☐

   (c) •••••••• + •••••••

   8 + ☐ = ☐

2. **Complete.**

   (a) ◯ ← +7   3 | 6   +7 → ◯ (b)
              7 | 9

   (c) ◯ ← +7   +7 → ◯ (d)

3.
(a)	(b)	(c)	(d)
1	7	11	0
+ 7	+ 7	+ 7	+ 7
☐	☐	☐	☐

4. **Count on 7.**

   (a) | 4 | ☐ | (b) | 7 | ☐ |

   (c) | 9 | ☐ | (d) | 12 | ☐ |

5. **Match.**

   (a) 5 + 7 •   17
   (b) 8 + 7 •   8
   (c) 12 + 7 •   19
   (d) 10 + 7 •   12
   (e) 1 + 7 •   15

   20

Test 8

1. (a) ••• + •••••

   5 + 8 = ☐

   (b) •••••• + •••••

   8 + 8 = ☐

   (c) ••••••• + •••••

   9 + ☐ = ☐

2.
(a)	(b)	(c)	(d)
2	7	9	11
+ 8	+ 8	+ 8	+ 8
☐	☐	☐	☐

3. (a) ⑤ + ⑧ = ☐
   (b) ⑧ + ⑧ = ☐
   (c) ⑫ + ⑧ = ☐
   (d) ⑩ + ⑧ = ☐

4.
	(a)	(b)	(c)	(d)	(e)
+	1	2	4	8	
8					18

5. **Match.**   +8

   (a) 2 •   • 13
   (b) 5 •   • 16
   (c) 8 •   • 19
   (d) 11 •   • 10

   20

Test 9

1. (a) $5 + 9 = \boxed{}$

(b) $7 + 9 = \boxed{}$

(c) $4 + 9 = \boxed{}$

2. (a) $2 + 9 = \boxed{}$

(b) $5 + 9 = \boxed{}$

(c) $8 + 9 = \boxed{}$

(d) $10 + 9 = \boxed{}$

3.
(a) $\begin{array}{r} 4 \\ + 9 \\ \hline \boxed{} \end{array}$
(b) $\begin{array}{r} 6 \\ + 9 \\ \hline \boxed{} \end{array}$
(c) $\begin{array}{r} 0 \\ + 9 \\ \hline \boxed{} \end{array}$
(d) $\begin{array}{r} 11 \\ + 9 \\ \hline \boxed{} \end{array}$

4. Ring the correct answer.

(a)	$3 + 9 =$	11	12	13
(b)	$6 + 9 =$	15	16	14
(c)	$8 + 9 =$	20	18	17
(d)	$10 + 9 =$	21	19	18

5. Match.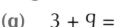

+ 9	
(a) 5•	•21
(b) 2•	•18
(c) 9•	•19
(d) 12•	•14
(e) 10•	•11

20

Test 10

1. (a) $5 + 10 = \boxed{}$

(b) $8 + 10 = \boxed{}$

(c) $\boxed{} + \boxed{} = \boxed{}$

2.

+	(a) 3	(b) 7	(c) 10	(d) 9	(e) 12
10					

3.
(a) $\begin{array}{r} 0 \\ + 10 \\ \hline \boxed{} \end{array}$
(b) $\begin{array}{r} 3 \\ + 10 \\ \hline \boxed{} \end{array}$
(c) $\begin{array}{r} 7 \\ + 10 \\ \hline \boxed{} \end{array}$
(d) $\begin{array}{r} 12 \\ + 10 \\ \hline \boxed{} \end{array}$

4. Complete.

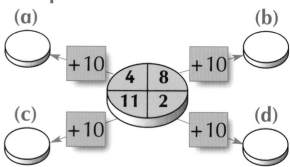

5. Complete. (Add.)

(a) $2 + 10 = \boxed{}$

(b) $\boxed{5} \quad \boxed{10} \quad \boxed{15}$

(c) $9 + \boxed{} = 19$

(d) $11 + \boxed{} \quad \boxed{21}$

20

Test 11

1. (a) ⬤⬤⬜⬤⬤⬤⬤⬤⬤ $3 + 11 = \boxed{}$

   (b) ⬤⬤⬤⬤⬤⬤⬤⬤⬤ $5 + 11 = \boxed{}$

   (c) ⬜⬤⬤⬤⬤⬤⬤⬤ $\boxed{} + \boxed{} = \boxed{}$

   (d) ⬤⬤⬤⬤⬤⬤⬜ $\boxed{} + \boxed{} = \boxed{}$

2.

(a)	(b)	(c)	(d)
4	6	10	12
+ 11	+ 11	+ 11	+ 11
$\boxed{}$	$\boxed{}$	$\boxed{}$	$\boxed{}$

3. (a) ① $+$ ⑪ $= \boxed{}$

   (b) ⑦ $+$ ⑪ $= \boxed{}$

   (c) ⑨ $+$ ⑪ $= \boxed{}$

   (d) ⑪ $+$ ⑪ $= \boxed{}$

   (e) ④ $+$ ⑪ $= \boxed{}$

4.

(a)   (b) $\boxed{}$ (c)

17   21

⋀   ⋀   ⋀

$6 + \boxed{}$ $4 + 11$ $11 + \boxed{}$

5. Match.

   (a) $1 + 11$ 19

   (b) $5 + 11$ •   22

   (c) $8 + 11$ •   12

   (d) $11 + 11$ •   16

$\boxed{}$ 20

Test 12

1. (a) ⬤⬤⬤ $+$ ⬤⬤⬤⬤⬤⬤⬤⬤

      $5 + 12 = \boxed{}$

   (b) ⬤⬤⬤ $+$ ⬤⬤⬤⬤⬤⬤⬤⬤

      $3 + 12 = \boxed{}$

   (c) ⬤⬤⬤⬤⬤⬤⬤⬤ $+$ ⬤⬤⬤⬤⬤⬤⬤⬤

      $8 + \boxed{} = \boxed{}$

2.

(a)	(b)	(c)	(d)
7	1	9	12
+ 12	+ 12	+ 12	+ 12
$\boxed{}$	$\boxed{}$	$\boxed{}$	$\boxed{}$

3.

	(a)	(b)	(c)	(d)
+	3	7	8	10
12				

4. Complete.

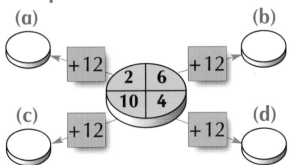

5. Complete. (Add.)

   (a) | 2 | + | 12 | = | $\boxed{}$ |

   (b) | 8 | | 12 | | 20 |

   (c) | 5 | | 12 | = | |

   (d) | 9 | | | = | 21 |

   (e) | 12 | + | | | 24 |

$\boxed{}$ 20

Tests Subtraction (– 1) to (– 4)

Test 13

1. (a) $5 - 1 = \boxed{}$

   (b) $9 - \boxed{} = \boxed{}$

   (c) $7 - \boxed{} = \boxed{}$

   (d) $10 - \boxed{} = \boxed{}$

2. Count back 1.

   (a) $\boxed{}\ 7$

   (b) $\boxed{}\ 9$

   (c) $\boxed{}\ 5$

   (d) $\boxed{}\ 8$

   (e) $\boxed{}\ 10$

   (f) $\boxed{}\ 12$

3.
   (a) $\begin{array}{r} 3 \\ -1 \\ \hline \boxed{} \end{array}$
   (b) $\begin{array}{r} 9 \\ -1 \\ \hline \boxed{} \end{array}$
   (c) $\begin{array}{r} 7 \\ -1 \\ \hline \boxed{} \end{array}$
   (d) $\begin{array}{r} 11 \\ -1 \\ \hline \boxed{} \end{array}$

4. Match.

   (a) $4 - 1$

   (b) $7 - 1$

   (c) $10 - 1$

   (d) $8 - 1$

   (e) $12 - 1$

   (f) $1 - 1$

   11
   9
   6
   0
   7
   3

   20

Test 14

1. (a) $8 - 2 = \boxed{}$

   (b) $6 - 2 = \boxed{}$

   (c) $10 - 2 = \boxed{}$

   (d) $9 - \boxed{} = \boxed{}$

2.
   (a) $\begin{array}{r} 8 \\ -2 \\ \hline \boxed{} \end{array}$
   (b) $\begin{array}{r} 5 \\ -2 \\ \hline \boxed{} \end{array}$
   (c) $\begin{array}{r} 3 \\ -2 \\ \hline \boxed{} \end{array}$
   (d) $\begin{array}{r} 9 \\ -2 \\ \hline \boxed{} \end{array}$

3. (a) $4 + \boxed{} = 6$, so $6 - 2 = \boxed{}$

   (b) $10 + \boxed{} = 12$, so $12 - 2 = \boxed{}$

   (c) $7 + \boxed{} = 9$, so $9 - 2 = \boxed{}$

   (d) $9 + \boxed{} = 11$, so $11 - \boxed{} = 9$

4. (a) $4 - 2 = \boxed{}$

   (b) $3 - 2 = \boxed{}$

   (c) $7 - 2 = \boxed{}$

   (d) $11 - 2 = \boxed{}$

5. Complete. (Subtract.)

   (a) | 6 | – | 2 | = | |

   (b) | 8 | | 2 | | 6 |

   (c) | 10 | – | | = | 8 |

   (d) | 12 | | 2 | | |

   20

1. (a) 7 − 3 = ☐

(b) 10 − ☐ = ☐

(c) 8 − ☐ = ☐

2. Complete.

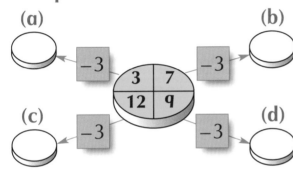

(a)

(b)

(c)

(d)

−3   −3   −3   −3

| 3 | 7 |
| 12 | 9 |

3.

(a)	(b)	(c)	(d)
4	8	3	11
− 3	− 3	− 3	− 3
☐	☐	☐	☐

4. (a) 2 + 3 = ☐, so 5 − 3 = ☐

(b) 6 + 3 = ☐, so 9 − 3 = ☐

(c) 9 + 3 = ☐, so 12 − 3 = ☐

(d) 12 + 3 = ☐, so 15 − 3 = ☐

5. Match.

(a) 6 − 3 •   5

(b) 10 − 3 •   8

(c) 8 − 3 •   3

(d) 11 − 3 •   0

(e) 3 − 3 •   7

20

1. (a) 10 − 4 = ☐

(b) 13 − 4 = ☐

(c) 9 − ☐ = ☐

2. (a) 10 − 4 = ☐

(b) 8 − 4 = ☐

(c) 9 − ☐ = ☐

(d) 14 − ☐ = ☐

3. Count back 4.

(a) ☐ | 7

(b) ☐ | 9

(c) ☐ | 4

(d) ☐ | 11

4.

(a)	(b)	(c)	(d)
6	10	4	7
− 4	− 4	− 4	− 4
☐	☐	☐	☐

5. (a) 7 − 4 = ☐

(b) 5 − 4 = ☐

(c) 8 − 4 = ☐

(d) 12 − 4 = ☐

(e) 9 − 4 = ☐

20

Tests Subtraction (– 5) to (– 8)

Test 17

1. (a) 8 – 5 = ☐

   (b) 11 – 5 = ☐

   (c) 13 – ☐ = ☐

   (d) 10 – ☐ = ☐

2. Complete.

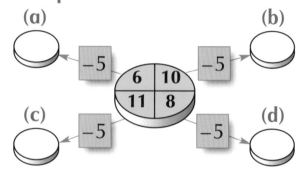

   (a)   (b)

   (c)   (d)

   –5   6 10
        11 8

3.
   (a) 7   (b) 9   (c) 5   (d) 12
      – 5   – 5   – 5   – 5
      ☐   ☐   ☐   ☐

4. Count back 5.

   (a) ☐ 8   (b) ☐ 6

   (c) ☐ 11   (d) ☐ 9

5. (a) 9 – 5 = ☐

   (b) 7 – 5 = ☐

   (c) 8 – 5 = ☐

   (d) 12 – 5 = ☐

   20

Test 18

1. (a) 8 – 6 = ☐

   (b) 10 – 6 = ☐

   (c) 11 – ☐ = ☐

   (d) 14 – ☐ = ☐

2.
   (a) 7   (b) 11   (c) 9   (d) 12
      – 6   – 6   – 6   – 6
      ☐   ☐   ☐   ☐

3. Ring the correct answer.

   (a) 8 – 6 = | 4 | 2 | 5
   (b) 7 – 6 = | 3 | 1 | 4
   (c) 12 – 6 = | 5 | 7 | 6

4. (a) 6 + ☐ = 6, so 6 – 6 = ☐

   (b) 6 + ☐ = 9, so 9 – 6 = ☐

   (c) 6 + ☐ = 12, so 12 – 6 = ☐

   (d) 6 + ☐ = 15, so 15 – 6 = ☐

5. Match.

– 6	
(a) 8•	• 0
(b) 10•	•10
(c) 6•	• 2
(d) 13•	• 4
(e) 16•	• 7

   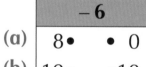

   20

Test 19

1. (a) 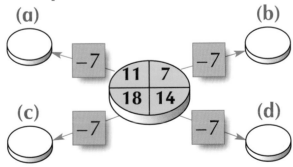 10 − 7 = ☐

   (b) 9 − 7 = ☐

   (c) 13 − ☐ = ☐

2.
(a)	(b)	(c)	(d)
8	11	7	14
− 7	− 7	− 7	− 7
☐	☐	☐	☐

3. (a) 9 − 7 = ☐

   (b) 16 − 7 = ☐

   (c) 12 − 7 = ☐

   (d) 15 − 7 = ☐

   (e) 17 − 7 = ☐

4. Complete.

   (a) ⊖ ← −7 11 | 7 / 18 | 14 −7 → ⊖ (b)

   (c) ⊖ ← −7   −7 → ⊖ (d)

5. Complete. (Subtract.)

   (a) | 8 | − | 7 | = | ☐ |

   (b) | 10 | | 7 | = | 3 |

   (c) | 13 | | 7 | = | ☐ |

   (d) | 16 | | | = | 9 |

   20

Test 20

1. (a) 12 − 8 = ☐

   (b) 14 − 8 = ☐

   (c) 10 − 8 = ☐

   (d) 16 − ☐ = ☐

2. Count back 8.

   (a) | ☐ | 9 | (b) | ☐ | 12 |

   (c) | ☐ | 15 | (d) | ☐ | 17 |

3.
(a)	(b)	(c)	(d)
8	14	11	16
− 8	− 8	− 8	− 8
☐	☐	☐	☐

4.
	− 8
(a) 10	
(b) 14	
(c) 16	
(d) 19	

5. Match.

   (a) 9 − 8   9

   (b) 12 − 8   0

   (c) 17 − 8   1

   (d) 8 − 8   4

   20

Test 21

1. (a) 14 – 9 = ☐

   (b) 11 – 9 = ☐

   (c) 16 – 9 = ☐

   (d) 13 – ☐ = ☐

2. (a) 12
      – 9
      ☐

   (b) 20
      – 9
      ☐

   (c) 10
      – 9
      ☐

   (d) 18
      – 9
      ☐

3. Count back 9.

   (a) ☐ | 10

   (b) ☐ | 13

   (c) ☐ | 16

   (d) ☐ | 19

4. (a) 9 + ☐ = 11, so 11 – 9 = ☐

   (b) 9 + ☐ = 14, so 14 – 9 = ☐

   (c) 9 + ☐ = 18, so 18 – 9 = ☐

   (d) 9 + ☐ = 20, so 20 – 9 = ☐

5. Fill in the gaps.

   (a) 12 – ⑨ ⇒ 3 + ② = ☐

   (b) 14 – ⑨ ⇒ ☐ – ④ = ☐

   (c) 20 – ⑨ ⇒ ☐ – ⑨ = ☐

   (d) 22 – ⑨ = ☐

   20

Test 22

1. (a) 14 – 10 = ☐

   (b) 20 – 10 = ☐

   (c) 18 – ☐ = ☐

   (d) ☐ – ☐ = ☐

2. Complete.

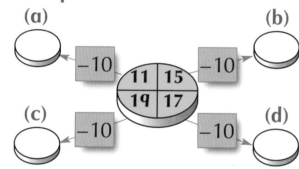

   (a) –10

   (b) –10

   (c) –10

   (d) –10

   11 | 15
   19 | 17

3. (a) 13 – 10 = ☐

   (b) 16 – 10 = ☐

   (c) 15 – 10 = ☐

   (d) 22 – 10 = ☐

4. (a) 12
      – 10
      ☐

   (b) 10
      – 10
      ☐

   (c) 17
      – 10
      ☐

   (d) 21
      – 10
      ☐

5. Match.

   (a) 11 – 10 •   9

   (b) 17 – 10 •   0

   (c) 10 – 10 •   1

   (d) 19 – 10 •   7

   20

Test 23

1. (a) [grid] 16 − 11 = [ ]

    (b) [grid] 18 − 11 = [ ]

    (c) [grid] 14 − 11 = [ ]

2.

(a)	(b)	(c)	(d)
14	11	19	22
− 11	− 11	− 11	− 11
[ ]	[ ]	[ ]	[ ]

3. Fill in the gaps.

    (a) [12] − (11) ⇒ [1] + (4) = [ ]

    (b) [17] − (11) ⇒ [ ] − (3) = [ ]

    (c) [19] − (11) ⇒ [ ] + (5) = [ ]

    (d) [22] − (11) ⇒ [ ] − (11) = [ ]

4. (a) 15 − [ ] = 4

    (b) 18 − 11 = [ ]

    (c) 23 − 11 = [ ]

    (d) 21 − [ ] = 10

5. (a) 12 − 11 = [ ]

    (b) 15 − 11 = [ ]

    (c) 17 − 11 = [ ]

    (d) 21 − 11 = [ ]

    (e) 19 − 11 = [ ]

    20

Test 24

1. Complete.

    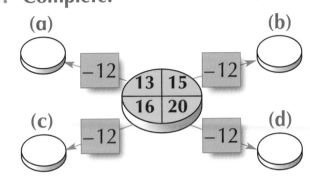

2.

(a)	(b)	(c)	(d)
14	17	12	19
− 12	− 12	− 12	− 12
[ ]	[ ]	[ ]	[ ]

3. Count back 12.

    (a) [ ] | 13   (b) [ ] | 16

    (c) [ ] | 20   (d) [ ] | 22

4. Match.

    (a) 12 − 12

    (b) 16 − 12 •

    (c) 20 − 12 •

    (d) 18 − 12 •

    8
    6
    0
    4

5. Complete. (Subtract.)

    (a) | 15 | − | 12 | = | [ ] |

    (b) | 18 | − | [ ] | = | 6 |

    (c) | 16 | [ ] | 12 | [ ] | 4 |

    (d) | 22 | − | [ ] | = | 10 |

    20

Record your **scores** on page **76**.

The Fifty Fivers   Addition

Name _____

Class _____

My time _____

Score _____

	A	**B**	**C**	**D**	**E**
1.	3 + 1 = ☐	1 + 2 = ☐	1 + 4 = ☐	1 + 3 = ☐	5 + 2 = ☐
2.	5 + 3 = ☐	3 + 4 = ☐	4 + 1 = ☐	6 + 2 = ☐	4 + 4 = ☐
3.	4 + 3 = ☐	3 + 2 = ☐	5 + 4 = ☐	3 + 3 = ☐	6 + 3 = ☐
4.	4 + 2 = ☐	5 + 1 = ☐	6 + 4 = ☐	7 + 2 = ☐	2 + 2 = ☐
5.	0 + 4 = ☐	2 + 5 = ☐	3 + 5 = ☐	2 + 6 = ☐	0 + 1 = ☐
6.	5 + 5 = ☐	3 + 6 = ☐	7 + 1 = ☐	5 + 6 = ☐	7 + 2 = ☐
7.	8 + 2 = ☐	6 + 4 = ☐	9 + 3 = ☐	10 + 5 = ☐	7 + 6 = ☐
8.	9 + 1 = ☐	8 + 3 = ☐	7 + 4 = ☐	9 + 6 = ☐	10 + 4 = ☐
9.	7 + 3 = ☐	12 + 1 = ☐	10 + 6 = ☐	11 + 4 = ☐	11 + 5 = ☐
10.	8 + 6 = ☐	7 + 5 = ☐	9 + 5 = ☐	11 + 3 = ☐	12 + 2 = ☐
11.	8 + 5 = ☐	11 + 6 = ☐	9 + 4 = ☐	12 + 5 = ☐	8 + 4 = ☐

Use the boxes below to rewrite the tables that you need to learn again.

1.					
2.					
3.					
4.					
5.					
6.					
7.					

The Fifty Fivers   Subtraction

Name _____   Class _____

My time _____   Score _____

	A	**B**	**C**	**D**	**E**
1.	2 – 1 = ☐	4 – 2 = ☐	2 – 2 = ☐	3 – 1 = ☐	4 – 3 = ☐
2.	7 – 7 = ☐	5 – 4 = ☐	4 – 1 = ☐	7 – 6 = ☐	3 – 2 = ☐
3.	5 – 5 = ☐	6 – 2 = ☐	5 – 3 = ☐	8 – 2 = ☐	6 – 4 = ☐
4.	5 – 1 = ☐	9 – 3 = ☐	7 – 5 = ☐	6 – 1 = ☐	8 – 6 = ☐
5.	8 – 4 = ☐	6 – 3 = ☐	7 – 2 = ☐	8 – 7 = ☐	7 – 3 = ☐
6.	9 – 5 = ☐	12 – 2 = ☐	8 – 3 = ☐	9 – 7 = ☐	11 – 6 = ☐
7.	10 – 3 = ☐	11 – 5 = ☐	9 – 6 = ☐	12 – 4 = ☐	10 – 7 = ☐
8.	9 – 9 = ☐	9 – 8 = ☐	12 – 3 = ☐	10 – 6 = ☐	9 – 4 = ☐
9.	11 – 3 = ☐	12 – 6 = ☐	10 – 8 = ☐	11 – 7 = ☐	7 – 1 = ☐
10.	12 – 10 = ☐	11 – 6 = ☐	9 – 2 = ☐	12 – 8 = ☐	8 – 5 = ☐
11.	11 – 8 = ☐	12 – 11 = ☐	10 – 4 = ☐	10 – 3 = ☐	11 – 9 = ☐

Use the boxes below to rewrite the tables that you need to learn again.

1.					
2.					
3.					
4.					
5.					
6.					
7.					

Test Scores	Pupil's name:	Class:

ADDITION

SUBTRACTION

	Test 1	Test 2	Test 3	Test 4	Test 5	Test 6	Test 7	Test 8	Test 9	Test 10	Test 11	Test 12	Test 13	Test 14	Test 15	Test 16	Test 17	Test 18	Test 19	Test 20	Test 21	Test 22	Test 23	Test 24
20.																								
19.																								
18.																								
17.																								
16.																								
15.																								
14.																								
13.																								
12.																								
11.																								
10.																								
9.																								
8.																								
7.																								
6.																								
5.																								
4.																								
3.																								
2.																								
1.																								

Total: /80	Total: /80	Total: /80	Total: /80	Total: /80	Total: /80

Make a bar graph of your scores.
Score yourself out of 20. **After each group of four tests,** score yourself out of 80.

76

	Revision A				Revision B				Revision C				Revision D				Revision E				Revision F			
	Revision 1	Revision 2	Revision 3	Revision 4	Revision 5	Revision 6	Revision 7	Revision 8	Revision 9	Revision 10	Revision 11	Revision 12	Revision 13	Revision 14	Revision 15	Revision 16	Revision 17	Revision 18	Revision 19	Revision 20	Revision 21	Revision 22	Revision 23	Revision 24
20.																								
19.																								
18.																								
17.																								
16.																								
15.																								
14.																								
13.																								
12.																								
11.																								
10.																								
9.																								
8.																								
7.																								
6.																								
5.																								
4.																								
3.																								
2.																								
1.																								

| Total: /80 | Total: /80 | Total: /80 | Total: /80 | Total: /80 | Total: /80 |

Make a bar graph of your scores.
Score yourself out of 20. **After each group of four tests,** score yourself out of 80.